SCHELLING: OF HUMAN FREEDOM

SCHELLING: OF HUMAN FREEDOM

A Translation of F. W. J. Schelling's *Philosophische Untersuchungen über das Wesen der menschlichen Freiheit und die damit zusammenhängenden Gegenstände* With a critical Introduction and Notes

By

JAMES GUTMANN, Ph.D.

Columbia University

CHICAGO

THE OPEN COURT PUBLISHING COMPANY

PRINTED IN THE UNITED STATES OF AMERICA

PREFACE

It seems probable that no other modern philosopher of an importance comparable to that of Schelling (the importance being indicated, perhaps, by the attention given him in any standard History of Philosophy) has been as little accessible to students unable to read his works in the original. The only translations into English of any of Schelling's writings are a 34-page pamphlet published in London in 1845, "The Philosophy of Art; an Oration on the Relation between the Plastic Arts and Nature," translated from the German by A. Johnson, and some fugitive papers published between 1867 and 1881 in the "Journal of Speculative Philosophy" in St. Louis by Thomas David son and others. In 1882 John Watson published his synoptic commentary, "Schelling's Transcendental Idealism."

In the decade following the war there seemed to be in Germany a marked revival of interest in Schelling. The publication of a new edition of Schelling's Collected Works, the compilation of a fifty page Bibliography of works by and about Schelling, as well as the appearance of a number of books and monographs on Schelling and the "Romantic School" made evident this revived interest. That this interest was not limited to Germany might be implied by the publication, in 1926, of a French translation of Schelling's *Philosophische Untersuchungen über das Wesen der menschlichen Freiheit und die damit zusammenhängenden Gegenstände,* the work which is presented in English translation in the present volume.

The selection of this work from among the voluminous writings of Schelling, I have attempted to explain and, perhaps, justify in the introductory essay. The "Inquiries" were published in 1809, a singularly fateful year in Schelling's life, and summarize, as it were, much of the thought of his earlier writing, as well as anticipating many of the interests and viewpoints characteristic of the last half of Schelling's lengthy career. A reading of this work would therefore seem to be a desirable approach to a study of Schelling's philosophy.

Moreover the subject of these "Inquiries" makes this essay a significant introduction not only to Schelling's thought but to many contemporary philosophers as well. The importance of the theme of freedom will be at once apparent to readers who are familiar with the Romantic Movement in the art and literature of the Nineteenth Century. How much this theme of freedom meant in Germany is evident to all who know the drama of Schiller or the music of Beethoven. Those who have cherished this noble tradition and have loved the German people whose contribution to it has been so great, may, even in these dark days, feel confident that it is not dead in Germany and will arise again to even nobler heights.

In contrast to the comparative brevity of the work here presented, the list of those who have assisted me is long indeed. My colleagues and friends in the Department of Philosophy of Columbia University, especially Professors John J. Coss, Irwin Edman, Horace L. Friess and John H. Randall Jr., have given me every possible encouragement. Particularly Professor Friess and Professor Fritz Marti of the University of Maryland have lavished their interest and care on the translation as though it were their own work, which, in a sense, it has become. At the beginning of my work I had the help of my friend Dr. Walther Eckstein of Vienna, whose own experience in translation from English into German made his counsel especially valuable; at that time I also benefitted by the kind advice of Dr. Manfred Schröter of Munich, editor of the new, still unfortunately incomplete, edition of Schelling's Collected Works, and by the interest of Dr. Werner Ziegenfuss who was, in 1930, in charge of the Philosophical Seminar Building of the University of Berlin, in whose then hospitable rooms I prepared the first draft of my translation.

On special points of difficulty I have had the generous help of Dr. James E. Frame of Union Theological Seminary; of Dr. F. W. J. Heuser, Professor of Germanic Languages and Literatures at Columbia; and of Mr. H. Theodric Westbrook of the Columbia Department of Classical Philology. I have received helpful suggestions from Professor Paul Tillich. My friend Dr. Jacques Barzun of the Department of History of Columbia University has added more than a mere acknowledgment can suggest to my understanding of the Romantic Movement.

Beyond these special obligations I have been aware, and not only in this single undertaking, of my constant indebtedness to three great teachers at whose feet I had the privilege of sitting: Felix Adler, John Dewey and Frederick J. E. Woodbridge. It would please me to think that their influence is discernible to others, as it often is to me, in the work that I have done.

My wife and my mother have helped to make less wearisome for me attention to innumerable details, as have my friends Lawrence W. Lamm and Neil C. Van Deusen, who have shared with me the burden of reading the proofs. To Carol S. Schneider I am indebted for aid in organizing the bibliography.

JAMES GUTMANN

Columbia University
March 31, 1936

CONTENTS

INTRODUCTION

I

PRINCE of the Romanticists is the pleasing epithet which Josiah Royce applied to Friedrich Wilhelm Joseph Schelling.[1] The title is suggestive; how far it is accurate we shall have occasion to consider later. That he was, however, something of a Prince, even a prince with the glamour of Romance about him, is indicated by the testimony of more than one of his contemporaries. They were "charmed" and "elevated" on first meeting him[2] and spoke of his "large, bright eyes wherein lay a spiritually commanding power."[3] Singularly gifted and endowed with powers of intellect and imagination which his generation esteemed above all others, he seems indeed to have been a kind of Prince Charming.

Born in Leonberg in Württemberg on January 27th, 1775, son of the pastor, Joseph Friedrich, and his wife, Gottlobin Marie, Schelling was not yet sixteen years old when, in 1790, he entered the theological seminary at Tübingen. Even then he possessed a "proud consciousness of his power" and of his "early ripened genius."[4] Hegel and

[1] *The Spirit of Modern Philosophy,* p. 181

[2] *Aus Schellings Leben. In Briefen.* I, p. 242. (Schelling's letters, edited, in three volumes, by G. L. Plitt. They are referred to below as: *Letters.*)

[3] *Letters,* I, p. 243.

[4] Dilthey, *Die Jugendgeschichte Hegels,* p. 13.

Hölderlin were his schoolmates at the seminary, and he was drawn to them by a common interest in the French Revolution; there is a story, probably apocryphal, of their setting up and dancing around a "Tree of Freedom" to celebrate the fall of the Bastille. As Schelling became more and more interested in "philosophy, there arose that youthful friendship between him and Hegel, so fateful to both of them."[5] His philosophic distinction was already established between the years 1794 and 1797, while he was a student at Tübingen and a young tutor. "The works of these years are already witnesses to his great philosophic gifts, he proceeds with rapid strides, sustained by a profound and thorough understanding" of Fichte's philosophy. He is "regarded as Fichte's ablest student, as the best exponent of his system (the *Wissenschaftslehre*) and as its 'second founder'."[6] So things stood when, in 1798, at the age of twenty-three, he was called to a professorship at the University of Jena.

The world which Schelling now entered with every prospect of becoming one of its ruling spirits was indeed a realm which a prince might envy. With Goethe and Schiller exercising their mighty influence at nearby Weimar, —a mere excursion drive across the hills where Schelling and his friends might go of a Saturday evening to witness a new dramatic production or to enjoy some other festive gathering,—with the much admired Fichte as inspiring colleague and friend at the University, with Hegel and Hölderlin as stimulating correspondents, and with the circle of artists and writers who gathered at the home of August and Caroline Schlegel as friendly acquaintances, his fortunes stood high indeed. Congenial surroundings, early fame,

[5] Dilthey, *Op. cit.* p. 13
[6] Kuno Fischer, *Schellings Leben, Werke, Lehre,* p. 281

and admiring approval of the recognized philosophic leader and of the undisputed spiritual master of his time, numerous gifted friends and ardent followers—all of these were his. Nor did he lack the romance of love. If this love was, apparently, a somewhat unimpassioned attachment to a young girl scarcely sixteen years of age, and if this maiden's untimely end involved the ugly accusation that his own untrained medical efforts had been largely responsible, it, nonetheless, followed in detail the accepted pattern of literary love as practised in the early years of the nineteenth century. Moreover, in Schelling's case, Fortune, as though to prove Prince Charming invincible, even at the death of his Princess, awarded him the hand of his Fairy Godmother. For Caroline Schlegel seems to have been precisely a Godmother-wife for Schelling. The circumstance that she had been the mother of the deceased Auguste, Schelling's sixteen year old beloved, was no more an obstacle than the fact that she was also the wife of his friend, August Wilhelm Schlegel.

The year of his marriage to Caroline, 1803, marked the end of the "Jena Period" of Schelling's life with all, or much, that it connoted in happy circumstances, inspiring companionship and stimulating friendships. The six years that followed, in Würzburg and Munich, though of course not altogether lacking in these goods and though filled by Caroline's wifely devotion, were comparatively years of isolation and embittered quarrels such as are reflected in the polemical passages of the *Inquiries into the Nature of Human Freedom.* This work appeared in 1809, the very year that brought to Schelling the blow of Caroline's death.

We can only guess what was the relation of this blow to the fact that though Schelling lived well over half of his life after Caroline's death—he died in 1854 at the ripe age of seventy-nine—and though he continued to write voluminously, the *Inquiries into the Nature of Human Freedom* was the last work of importance published during his lifetime. The last forty-five years of his life were filled with much work and with much domestic felicity; in 1812 Schelling married a friend of Caroline's, Pauline Gotter, who bore him a large family. But neither domestic joy nor the literary and academic conflicts which continued to fill these years, nor even the significant work which they witnessed, would seem to justify the title of Prince of Romanticists. The Prince must be found, if at all, in the years previous to 1810.

And there he should be found not only in his princely personality and fortunes, as just sketched, but in his works. These appeared, during the years in Jena, with almost phenomenal rapidity. In 1798 and 1799 he published his *First Plan of a System of Natural Philosophy* as well as the independent and comprehensive *Introduction* to this work. *The General Deduction of the Dynamic Process* appeared in 1800 as well as the famous *System of Transcendental Idealism.* 1801 witnessed the *Presentation of my System of Philosophy* and 1802 the dialogue entitled *Bruno.* The *Lectures on the Method of University Study* were published in 1803. These numerous works together with other published lectures, such as the important *Lectures on Art,* and many occasional writings, are the products of the Jena period.

The years from 1803 to 1809 were less productive. But in 1804 appeared the *Philosophy of Religion* and, in 1806, the *Exposition of the True Relation of the Philosophy of Nature to the Improved Doctrine of Fichte.* To this year also belong a number of contributions to the *Annuals of Medicine as a Science,* referred to in the *Inquiries into the Nature of Human Freedom.* In 1807 Schelling gave an address, republished in 1809 together with the *Inquiries,* on the *Relation of the Plastic Arts to Nature.* And in 1809 as the fifth essay in a volume of *Philosophical Writings,* intended as the first of a series, though never continued, appeared the *Philosophical Inquiries into the Nature of Human Freedom and Matters connected therewith.*

Thus 1809 marks, in a number of ways, a climax in Schelling's life and works. His failure to follow the intention of publishing additional volumes of his *Philosophical Writings* as well as his neglect of the promise contained in the last paragraph of the *Inquiries,* suggests that here was a premature conclusion to Schelling's career. In a sense this is true, and it may also be held that the *Inquiries* summarized much of Schelling's earlier work. They also anticipated some of the interests of his later years, and, perhaps for this reason, shared the lack of attention given to these writings.

II

The markedly disputatious and sharply polemical passages of the *Inquiries* will strike the attention of most readers. This is a quality characteristic of Schelling, to be found in almost all of his writings and even more evident in some other works than in the present text. That Schelling carried a chip on his philosophic shoulder is apparent; his son and biographer penetratingly suggests that this attitude may have been connected with the circumstances of his student years at the seminary, when he was together with fellow students so much older than himself whom, nonetheless, he so greatly excelled. That this circumstance "was not quite wholesome for him" and that it is connected with "the tendency to take pleasure in exposing the ridiculous or castigating what was mediocre" seems probable, and certainly "the tendency was deeply rooted in him."[7]

Be that as it may, the sharply argumentative strain appeared in his philosophic writings very early, and even before going to Jena he felt called upon to "silence all his literary opponents of whom many had already grown dumb," as he wrote his parents from Leipzig in November 1797, assuring them that his "philosophic principles were gaining influence."[8]

Purely personal, non-philosophic factors entered frequently into these disputes. The most spectacular was the unpleasant argument concerning his supposed responsibility for the death of Caroline's daughter, though, to be sure, there were here involved questions concerning Schelling's medical theories and related doctrines. Also connected with this dispute were elements of scandal in his subsequent marriage to Caroline, following her divorce from Schlegel.

Many of his public debates were carried on against former friends. In his relations to his friends he seems to have demanded the utmost intellectual as well as personal loyalty, not to say subservience. One after another, friendships were sacrificed to his exaggerated pride. This was true of his relation to Hegel, Fichte, Schlegel, Jacobi, and a host of less famous contemporaries as well,—Paulus, Röschlaub, Eschenmayer, Windischmann, and many others. His correspondence at the time of a quarrel with the last named, reveals the extent to which Schelling could go in his savage intolerance of all criticism. This quarrel, on the other hand, was almost unique in that the breach was presently allowed to heal, due doubtless to Windischmann's

[7] *Letters,* I, p. 22
[8] *Letters,* I, p. 210

extraordinary forbearance, so that he was honored by Schelling with the request to review the *Inquiries into the Nature of Human Freedom.* "Friend" and "enemy" alike were subject to his onslaughts, as witness his antagonism to "uninvited supporters as well as hostile critics."

On the other hand it must not be imagined that the critics were lacking or too delicate in their attentions. In his early fame Schelling shared the obloquy visited upon Fichte by the self-appointed guardians of orthodoxy. These continued their attacks throughout the years of Schelling's residence in Jena and even longer. During his years in Würzburg, from 1803 to 1806, he was, as a matter of fact, under fire from two diametrically opposed camps. In the first place, the representatives of the "Enlightenment" in Bavaria, led by Salat and Cogitan Weiller, and cooperating with Schelling's Würzberg colleague, Berg, attacked him as a representative of religious obscurantism dangerous to the "Enlightenment" which was just becoming effective in Bavaria. On the other hand the spokesmen of Catholicism opposed him as dangerous to the Church.[9]

At least one phrase in the *Philosophical Inquiries into the Nature of Human Freedom* makes it evident that Schelling himself was not only willing to accept the challenge of lesser philosophic opponents but that he urged comparison with the greatest as well. "The thought of making Freedom the one and all of Philosophy has emancipated the human spirit in all its relationships and not only in respect to itself; and has given to science in all its parts a more powerful reorientation than any earlier revolution."[10] Clearly

[9] *Letters,* II, pp. 2-5

[10] *Schellings Sämmtliche Werke,* VII, p. 351. (Schelling's works edited, in fourteen volumes, by his son, K. F. A. Schelling. They are referred to below as: *Works.* All citations from volume VII, pp. 333-416 will, of course, be found in the translation below.)

he was writing as a new leader of this revolution, inviting comparison even with the "Copernican Revolution" of Kant himself.

In politics an unsuccessful revolutionary is likely to be reproached as a "rebel" while his successful followers take the laurels. In philosophy he is given the milder epithet of "forerunner" or, more impersonal, "transition." Thus Schelling, in the one slim volume written in English about him, is treated as being essentially "the transition from Kant to Hegel through Fichte."[11] Writing in the heydey of what might be called the Hegelian revival in America, Watson argued that "the best fruit of the study of Schelling is the hold it enables us to have over the infinitely richer and fuller system of his successor Hegel."[12] This disposition to regard Hegel as Schelling's "successor" is an historical anachronism which appears to overlook the facts of their philosophies, to say nothing of the circumstance that Schelling was Hegel's younger schoolmate and survived him by more than twenty years. It is justified chiefly by another tradition, namely, that all of Schellings' significant writing preceded Hegel's; but whether this view is itself justifiable is another question. Certainly it is the basis of such a judgment, or prejudice, that "Schelling is only Hegel in germ and Hegel with much that is most valuable in him left out."[13]

At the opposite extreme from this view we find the conviction expressed by Schelling that whatever he and Hegel had in common was plagiarism in Hegel. This conviction was immortalized by Heinrich Heine in his description of one of Schelling's utterances on the subject, which

[11] Watson, *Schelling's Transcendental Idealism,* p. 3
[12] *Ibid.* p. 251
[13] *Ibid.* p. 193

Heine witnessed: "Just as a cobbler speaks of another cobbler whom he accuses of having stolen his leather and having made boots out of it, so I heard Mr. Schelling, when by chance I once met him, speak about Hegel. He had 'taken his ideas' from him and 'they are my ideas which he has taken', and again, 'my ideas' was the perpetual chorus of the poor man."[14]

The personal relations of Schelling and Hegel were, of course, such as to make difficult any determination of precise obligation, for during their early, philosophically formative years they studied together and their friendship seems indeed to have been "based more on intellectual than on social congeniality."[15] Later they collaborated and from 1802 to 1804 they were co-editors of the *Critical Journal of Philosophy.* Their correspondence reveals not only the genuineness of this intellectual congeniality but also an unwillingness on Schelling's part to believe that the passages of Hegel's *Phenomenology,* published in 1807, which contained sharp criticism were intended to refer to him, preferring "as you (Hegel) have indicated in your letter, to apply them only to false use (of Schelling's ideas) and loose-tongued imitators, although in the work itself no such distinction is made."[16] And in the last letter which passed between the two, in November 1807,[17] Schelling urges reconciliation by discovering "those things in which we really have different convictions or opinions." After Hegel's death, Schelling, who survived him by more than a score of years, spoke of Hegel's work and of his own early writing as having been a "negative philosophy" which was

[14] *Die Romantische Schule. Heines Sämmtliche Werke* (Leipzig, 1910) VII, p. 9
[15] *Letters,* I, p. 69
[16] *Letters,* I, p. 179
[17] *Letters,* II, pp. 123-4

to be completed by his later "positive philosophy."[18]

Schelling's relations to Fichte were also complicated. In this case there is no doubt as to Schelling's initial obligation and, indeed, discipleship. This was freely acknowledged by him,[19] and in his preface to the first edition of his work on *The Ego,* published in 1795, he wrote, "It has been reserved for but few, perhaps for but one, to usher in a brighter day for science."[20] But though Fichte was the "one," there is no question that Schelling regarded himself as among the "few" collaborators. And Fichte himself recognized this relationship, when in 1799, at the time of his departure from Jena, he wrote: "It would have been fine indeed if I had been able to go on working with Schelling."[21] That by 1809 there was no longer any discipleship or even complete acceptance of the Fichtean system is evident in explicit references in the *Inquiries.*

His relations to the group called Romanticists were hardly less complicated. Whether Heinrich Heine exaggerated when he wrote that Schelling's "influence on the 'Romantic School' was chiefly of the personal kind,"[22] he was in close contact with many of them. Though he had never felt personally close to Friedrich Schlegel and though, as several footnotes to the *Inquiries into the Nature of Human Freedom* indicate, he showed scant sympathy with certain of Schlegel's doctrines, particularly those related to pantheism, he had been intimate with most of the group who composed the German "Romantic School." August Wilhelm Schlegel

[18] *Cf.* Schelling's introduction to Victor Cousin's *Essays on French and German Philosophy,* translated into German by Hubert Beckers, 1834; and Schelling's Inaugural Address at Berlin, 1841.

[19] *Cf.* below, section IV

[20] *Works,* I, pp. 149-244

[21] *Letters,* I, p. 245

[22] Heine, *op. cit.,* p. 104

and Schelling were "inseparable" as Caroline wrote[23] even after her divorce from the former and marriage to the latter. Ludwig Tieck, with whom he shared an interest in folk-lore and especially (perhaps in part through Tieck's influence)[24] an enthusiasm for the writings of Jacob Böhme, he admired for his talents as a dramatic reader: "one can think of no more royal treat than to hear him read and improvise a comedy,"[25] wrote Schelling. Novalis who admired Schelling's "radiant power,"[26] he, in turn, seems to have liked but not trusted, at least in intellectual matters.[27] Though not resident in Jena, Hölderlin, Schelling's old schoolmate and friend, may be considered one of the Romanticists, and Schleiermacher, whose admirer Schelling declared himself to be,[28] belonged to their group.

Goethe, although not considered a member of the "Romantic School" was in close contact with the group at Jena. His own letters to Schelling seem hardly more than cordial, but at least in Caroline's loving fancy the relationship was far more intimate. "Goethe," she wrote to Schelling in October 1800, "resigns poetry to you, he transmits his genius to you. Since he cannot make you his heir he makes a donation to you among the living. He loves you as a father, I love you as a mother—what wonderful parents you have."[29]

To say what common characteristics made these men—Tieck, Novalis, the Schlegels, Hölderlin, Schleiermacher—members of the "Romantic School," would be far from

[23] *Letters,* II, p. 89
[24] *Letters,* I, p. 247
[25] *Letters,* II, p. 137
[26] Novalis' letter to Friedrich Schlegel, December 26, 1797. Quoted by Stefansky, *Das hellenisch-deutsche Weltbild,* p. 125
[27] *Letters,* I, pp. 431-2
[28] *Letters,* I, p. 345
[29] *Karoline* (letters of Caroline Schlegel-Schelling) II, p. 3

easy. That they themselves were at least as keenly conscious of elements in their characters and convictions which distinguished them from one another as of those which bound them together, is a commonplace. It is often only from the vantage point of historical retrospect that the common characteristics of such a group are discernible, and then the perspective very possibly involves distortion. If it is true of most groups that they are more aware of and more interested in the attitudes and ideas which distinguish each from the others than in commonly accepted viewpoints, this was true to an altogether special degree of the Romanticists since they particularly esteemed differences of personality, all that was distinct or unique, as the mark of genius.

Romanticism has often been described as a protest or reaction against the age which preceded it,—the Age of Enlightenment, the Age of Reason. There are, of course, elements of truth in this description. Yet by making the factor of "reaction" or "protest" the central theme, the opposition aspect may well have been exaggerated and the positive content of the Romantic Movement inadequately regarded. There was among the romanticists not a rejection of Science though there was constant criticism of the mechanistic theories of the 18th century. There was certainly no general protest against Reason, though there was criticism of rationalistic dogmas in religion, for example, or ethics. To oppose Rationalism is, however, hardly the same as to reject reason. To deny mechanism is not equivalent to denying the importance of science.

Let us trace the thoughts of Schelling on the themes of science and religion, of faith and morals, as revealed in the *Inquiries,* in the attempt to discover some of the attitudes and ideas, positive as well as critical, which a "romantic" philosopher expressed on these fundamentals.

In the very beginning of the Preface to the *Inquiries,* he advances the thought, a favorite point in all his earlier works on the Philosophy of Nature, that it is false to characterize nature as mechanistic.[30] Such an approach will never yield that insight and understanding which is the object of genuine science.[31] Later in the *Inquiries* Schelling similarly rejects the doctrine of "emanationism" on the score that it seeks to explain the origin of creatures "as a mechanical production."[32] He denies that Spinoza's philosophy rightly understood implies that a system of reason must be mechanistic, and finds the fatalism which he rejects rooted in Spinoza's "abstract conception of Nature,"[33] in which "Things are mere things, lifeless and passive, and which he (Schelling) would correct through a more elevated way of regarding Nature."[34] It is not, he says later on returning to this theme, the doctrine of Immanence which is to be criticised but the "lifeless" conception of a relationship which merely "includes Things in God."[35] Creation is not passive, and a complete philosophy of nature must illustrate with the "dynamic mode of explanation" this constant activity "becoming" by showing how, in a graded evolution "each successive process more clearly approaches the essence of nature."[36]

It should not be thought that the rejection of mechanistic

[30] *Works,* VII, p. 333. Cf. translation below. All subsequent references in this Introduction, unless otherwise noted, are to the *Inquiries into the Nature of Human Freedom etc., Works,* VII, pp. 333-416, the pagination of which is indicated in the margin of the translation below.

[31] p. 335

[32] p. 347

[33] p. 348

[34] p. 350

[35] p. 358

[36] p. 362

theories implies opposition to the conception of Natural Law. System in nature is to be found throughout creation, but this is not lacking in the element of struggle, nor is the order which laws of nature describe made by these laws. Though there is order in nature, "the unruly lies ever in the depths."[37] The Heraclitean strife which this involves is analogous to the conflicts in the body in health and disease.[38] Disease follows laws although it is disruptive of the unity of the order of the body. Laws describe what happens, they do not determine it. It was not only the search for the wrong kind of laws which misled earlier science, but the wrong kind of search, dependent upon the mechanistic hypothesis. "Otherwise geometric reasoning which has ruled so long, must long since have fully penetrated Nature and have achieved its idol of universal and eternal laws of nature more fully than has yet occurred."[39]

In his moral teaching Schelling would not reject the important place which rationalistic ethics had given to the intellect, but he would correct the identification of passion with vice, and introduce the all-important concept of personality. He holds it a fundamental mistake to identify evil with the world of the senses and to regard moral freedom merely "as the mastery of the intelligent principle over the desires and inclination of the senses."[40] Animality is in itself neither good nor evil, and hence he holds Franz Baader "right in saying that it would be desirable that the rottenness in man could only go so far as animality, but unfortunately man can only stand above or beneath the animals."[41]

[37] p. 359
[38] p. 366
[39] p. 396
[40] p. 371
[41] p. 373

Indeed passion and desire are the *sine qua non* of freedom in nature as in man[42] This is consistent with Schelling's rejection of the conception of freedom as the passionless preference—or acceptance—of either of two alternatives, and his identification of it with an "inner necessity"[43] But this is no doctrine of easy optimism. Evil as well as desire is inherent in man. "All who are born are born with the dark principle of evil attached to them . . . Only he could gainsay this original evil in man who has but superficially come to know man in himself and others . . ." But "it is not the passions which are themselves evil."[44] To neglect the essential relation of passion to virtue is to accept a merely negative morality. "Activated selfhood is necessary for life's intensity . . . Goodness without effective selfhood is itself an ineffective Goodness."[45]

The term "personality" is central to Schelling's religious ideology as well as his ethics, indeed he expressed the conviction that he had established the first distinct conception of divine personality, in contrast to his critics and "accusers" who could only say that "God's personality is incomprehensible" because they based their views on "abstract systems."[46] In regard to this, at least, Schelling preferred to align himself with those "mystics and religious temperaments in all ages" who found their initial wisdom in God.[47] Their appeal to faith was, so to speak, reinforced by the advent of Idealism which made it evident that a system of reason need not lack all appeal to the heart and

[42] p. 376
[43] p. 385
[44] p. 388
[45] p. 400
[46] p. 412
[47] pp. 339, 415. On Schelling's general view of the relation of philosophy and theosophy, *cf.* below section V.

to faith.[48] The essential conception of the personality of God is furthermore strengthened by the conviction of the theologians that "God must become Man in order that man may be brought back to God," for "only Personality can make whole what is personal."[49]

Although Schelling returns to the thought of his earlier writings[50] in denying that religion is to be based on morality or that the idea of God is dependent upon or to be deduced from ethical considerations, he affirms that "religiosity" in its original and practical meaning is conscientiousness "in the highest sense of the word" as it appears in "strict performance of duty."[51] Moreover religiosity is not to be confused with sentimental enthusiasm or "idle brooding" and "pietistic intimations" of Divinity.[52] Rather faith, in its original significance of trust and confidence in what is divine is expressed in adherence to "the divine principle of morality."[53]

This does not deny the importance of Revelation, for that which is morally necessary in God "also follows with a genuine metaphysical necessity."[54] Schelling expresses agreement with Lessing's *Education of the Human Race* and holds that the exposition of the truths of Revelation as truths of Reason is the task of the philosopher.[55] To this task he devoted the posthumously published works of the latter half of his life,—the *Philosophies of Mythology and Revelation.*

[48] p. 348
[49] p. 380
[50] E.g. *Philosophy and Religion,* Works, VI, especially pp. 53-55; and the *System of Philosophy as a Whole,* Works, VI, especially p. 557.
[51] pp. 392-393
[52] p. 392
[53] p. 394
[54] p. 397
[55] p. 412

The consideration of "romantic elements" in Schelling's philosophy is further complicated by the tradition which holds that there was no such thing as Schelling's philosophy, that he had many philosophies.

III

The tradition which regards Schelling as the Proteus among the philosophers started early and may well have been stimulated by Hegel's scorn of his former friend and philosophic rival who "carried on his philosophic education before the public, and signalized each fresh stage of his advance by a new treatise." Certainly the echo of this judgment is heard in the above quoted essay by Josiah Royce when he asserts that "Schelling possesses directly the wavering passion of his romantic friends" and that his "kaleidoscopic philosophy, which changed form with each new essay he published, was like their whole scheme of life and art."[56] The judgment, or prejudice, which this statement implies concerning the romantic viewpoint and way of life deserves further questioning, but it clearly implies that this "romanticism" was related to intellectual instability in Schelling.

Historians of philosophy have thus been at pains to discover into how many "periods" Schelling's work could be divided. Windelband distinguished five periods.[57] Zeller recognized four, as did Kuno Fischer[58] whereas Eduard von

[56] *The Spirit of Modern Philosophy,* p. 173.
[57] *Geschichte der Philosophie.*
[58] Zeller, *Geschichte der deutschen Philosophie seit Leibniz;* Fischer, *Schellings Leben, Werke und Lehre.*

Hartmann and Drews[59] were each content with two divisions,—from 1797 to 1806 and from 1806 to 1854. Nicolai Hartmann,[60] like Windelband, discerns five periods and, also like Windelband, he places the "Philosophy of Freedom" as fourth.

In contrast to these historians we may cite the judgment of two other students of Schelling. Heinrich Lisco writes that "Schelling was more consistent in his development than the usual view assumes, but . . . this consistency is more in persistent problems than in adherence to (the same) solutions."[61] This view seems to persist in quite literal form for a more recent writer[62] makes the same distinction: "Schelling's development was more consistent than is commonly assumed. We may express it reasonably by saying that, in general, the problems are the constants and their solutions the variable elements." This judgment may be confirmed to a degree by reference to the problem of the nature of freedom, though if any philosophic integrity is to be found in an author, one might hope that it would be in something more than a preoccupation with persistent problems.

Even those who, like Windelband and Nicolai Hartmann, place Schelling's "Philosophy of Freedom" in a separate and specific "period" of his development, must recognize that the problem of the nature of freedom was of interest to him in all his various "periods." It may not be necessary to argue that the thought of freedom is for Schelling "the one and all, which he grasps with utter passion" or that

[59] v. Hartmann, *Geschichte der Metaphysik,* II; Drews, *Die Philosophie im ersten Drittel des 19ten Jahrhunderts.*

[60] *Die Philosophie des deutschen Idealismus,* I.

[61] *Die Geschichtsphilosophie Schellings,* p. 4.

[62] Paul Genths, *Die Identitätsphilosophie Schellings in ihrem Verhältnis zur Religion*, p. 11.

"all else, the whole System of Idealism and the whole Critical Philosophy are only of importance to him as the foundation and defence of this one thought and as a weapon against everything that endangers it."[63] But whether or not one agrees with this, it may be easily demonstrated that Schelling's interest in Freedom was not limited to the "period" of the "Philosophy of Freedom."

Schelling's method throughout his life was to take apparently contradictory terms and ideas and to show that they could be distinguished and differentiated without being viewed as conflicting. His passion for making distinctions was equalled, or perhaps exceeded, by the passion to reconcile them, to find unity amidst diversity. The distinctions which Schelling used were determined in large measure, as such distinctions are likely to be, by the interests and problems of chief concern in the European philosophical situation of his day. Thus they were, however remote they may appear in expression, largely the result of the cultural needs and setting of his age and of the philosophic preoccupations of his time. Accordingly they varied from time to time, or, at least, were given varying accent and emphasis. The problem of freedom as expounded by Schelling seldom seems directly relevant to the social and political difficulties of the early nineteenth century, yet the centrality of this problem and interest for Schelling, as well as for many of his contemporaries, can hardly be divorced from the repercussions of the French Revolution and of its libertarianism.[64]

It is the constancy of the concern to adjust, harmonize, reconcile by discovering a basis of unity, identity, indifference in which apparent contradictions are eliminated, that marks not only his "Philosophy of Identity," but all Schel-

[63] Emil Fuchs, *Vom Werden dreier Denker,* pp. 190-191.
[64] *Cf.* for instance, *Works,* I, p. 243.

ling's works. In the elimination of these apparent contradictions, the valid differences which distinguished the separate elements were never to be lost sight of, and the relation of the factor of unity to the factor of diversity (itself, in a sense, one of the prime "oppositions") remained another constant throughout Schelling's writings.

Though at one point in the *Inquiries* he argues that God's will universalizes, whereas the "will of the Deep," particularizes everything,[65] in general the contrasting factors of unity and diversity are taken as unexplained and, presumably, inexplicable elements basic to all thought. Indeed it is only by the separation of forces within unity that "reason can unfold and develop."[66] Nor is the unity to be taken as more fundamental, itself underived.[67] Differentiation and distinction are the necessary counterparts to unity and are not to be identified with discord which is itself a false unity.[68] Moreover, just as differentiation as well as unity is required in thinking, they are both also necessary so that there may be genuine life.[69] In Nature, by "graded evolution," there is developed "a new being whose soul must be all the more perfect the more differentiatedly it contains what was left undifferentiated in others."[70]

But this Nature within which differentiation takes place, is itself a term of distinction, an element of unity. The distinction between Nature and Spirit with which Schelling opens his Preface to the *Inquiries,* is fundamental for him, but at the very outset he disputes the validity of the contrast as usually conceived, since it had been based upon

[65] p. 381
[66] p. 361
[67] p. 359
[68] pp. 370-371
[69] p. 376
[70] p. 362

the traditional view of Nature as mechanistic. A valid Philosophy of Nature must recognize the distinction between "being as existence" and "being as the mere basis of existence," which also involves "the most definite distinction between Nature and God."[71] Insisting on these distinctions, Schelling seeks to meet the charge of "Pantheism" which had been brought against him, and to refute the accusation that he had confounded God with his creatures. Pantheism, he argues, contrary to its critics, does not "identify" God with all things but is the very doctrine of differentiation between Things and God.[72] To assert that "the Perfect is the Imperfect" does not signify the equivalence of perfection and imperfection, any more than to say that Evil is Good (really meaning that Evil has no power to exist by itself) denies the eternal difference between right and wrong. All such errors are due to the misapplication of the Law of Identity, and the misunderstanding of the nature of the copula. Even in apparent tautologies the relation of the subject and predicate is the relation of the term considered first in its unity, then in its individual qualities.[73] Thus, just as Pantheism rightly understood, does not fail to recognize that God is not equivalent to the totality of things, it is also not guilty in asserting the unity of God, of arguing that "Things are naught."[74] For Pantheism, as for any other system, though all things are conceived as dependent on the Eternal, as the ground of their existence, this does not exclude the autonomy or even the independence of things.[75] Unity is of the essence, but so is diversity.

"Every being which arises in Nature contains a double

[71] pp. 357-358
[72] p. 340
[73] p. 342
[74] p. 343
[75] p. 346

Principle which, however, is at bottom one and the same."[76] The Principle of Darkness must be sharply distinguished from the Principle of Light, though the former can only be revealed in the latter,[77] and attains its full significance only when it has "been born to Light as in Man."[78] "For every nature can be revealed only in its opposite—Love in Hatred, Unity in Strife."[79] Even God requires such a duality, but for God the differentiated principle or basis "is not outside of him, but within him."[80]

At "the highest point of the whole inquiry" Schelling reaches a conception which is presented as being antecedent to all duality.[81] The realm of the Ungrounded (*Ungrund*) precedes all antitheses, and since this is so it cannot even be designated in terms of Identity but only of Indifference. "Indifference is not a product of antitheses, nor are they implicitly contained in it, but it is a unique being apart from all antitheses, in which all distinctions break up."[82] This last phrase would surely seem to indicate, then, that at this point, the "highest point," the making of distinctions was to be impossible. But, no. There is a distinction between the term "Duality" and "Antithesis," "though we may have used the two as meaning the same thing up to the present"[83] and this distinction permits an important comment on the nature of "Indifference" itself. For though all antitheses are lacking in Indifference, and though even the primal principles, "Darkness and Light, or however else we wish to designate the two principles, can never be

[76] p. 362
[77] p. 362
[78] p. 372
[79] p. 374
[80] p. 375
[81] p. 406
[82] p. 406
[83] p. 407

predicated of the Ungrounded *as an antithesis*," there is nothing to prevent "their being predicated as non-antitheses, that is, in disjunction and each *for itself;* wherein, however, this duality (the real two-foldness of the principles) is established."[84]

Thus Schelling seeks to validate duality without dualism. Here is the union of Realism and Idealism of which he writes: "Idealism is the soul of Philosophy; Realism is its body; only the two together constitute a living whole."[85]

IV

That Schelling, at least in retrospect, thought of the theme of Freedom as the central one in his philosophy from the beginning, is evident in the posthumously published work on the history of modern philosophy[86] contained in an Erlangen manuscript of 1822, composed when Schelling was nearing fifty and was already at work on his last writings. Speaking of his first work he said that "the task which I first set myself was the following: to explain the concept of an objective world which is altogether independent of our Freedom, and indeed limits our Freedom, through reference to the process in which the ego, through the very act of positing itself, is implicated in an unintended but necessary way."[87] The obviously Fichtean terminology as well as thought of this statement is frankly acknowledged by Schelling in reiterating the centrality of his interest in Freedom. "I wished at that time only to explain Fichte's

[84] p. 407
[85] p. 356
[86] *Works*, X, pp. 1-200
[87] *Works*, X, pp. 96-97

system, though I had never been a regular member of his classes, which I mention only as a matter of history and not indeed to rid myself of the obligation to Fichte or to deny him as teacher and predecessor. For he was that to me as he was to all others, insofar as he first gave utterance to a Philosophy based upon Freedom, on the independence of the ego, not merely, as in Kant, on practical freedom but also on theoretic independence upon which, accordingly, the whole of philosophy rested."[88]

In 1795 he had written: "The whole of knowledge has no status if it is not supported by some thing which maintains itself by its own power, and this is nothing but that which is real through Freedom. The beginning and end of all philosophy is—Freedom."[89] This Freedom, Schelling holds, is an axiomatic fundamental of philosophy which does not need to be proved. "Philosophy he holds to be a pure product of a free human being, and itself an act of Freedom . . . He believes that man is born to act and not to speculate, and that thus his very first step in philosophy must proclaim the appearance of a free being. The first postulate of all philosophy, to act freely in its own terms, seemed as necessary to him as the first postulate of geometry, to draw a straight line. Just as little as the geometrician proves the line, should the philosopher prove Freedom."[90]

In this work, in the attempt to define the ego itself, he asserted: "*Its essence is Freedom,* that is the ego cannot be conceived except insofar as it posits itself through its absolute power as pure ego and not as any *Thing.* This Freedom may be positively determined for we wish to

[88] *Works,* X, p. 96
[89] *Works,* I. p. 177
[90] *Works,* I, pp. 242-3

ascribe Freedom not to any thing-in-itself but to an Ego which is pure and autonomous, present to itself and excluding all non-ego."[91]

In the same year, 1795, in which this essay on the Ego was written, Schelling stated in his *Philosophic Letters on Dogmatism and Criticism*: "The time has come to proclaim to a nobler humanity the freedom of the spirit, and no longer to have patience with men's tearful regrets for their lost chains."[92] The chains here referred to were the chains of theological "obscurantism" and "superstition" imposed by those who refused to meet Schelling on the "battlefield of reason" but sought "to fell him in the back-alleys of superstition."[93] To save intellectual freedom from them was Schelling's expressed object, for "the highest dignity of Philosophy consists precisely therein, that it stakes all on human freedom. Nothing can be so injurious to Philosophy as the attempt to force it into the bounds of a system of theoretically universal applicability."[94] The distinction between a philosophical system making claims to such universal applicability and one which, by contrast, does justice to individuality is here recognized, and Schelling insists that the more a system of philosophy approaches the truth, "the more will Freedom and Individuality have a part in it and the less will it lay claim to universal applicability."[95]

In these *Letters* the theme of Freedom is recurrent but the mood often differs from that of the *Inquiries*. The *Letters* end on a note of Promethean stoicism: "One thing remains: to know that there is an objective Power which

[91] *Works*, I, p. 179
[92] *Works*, I, p. 292
[93] *Works*, I, p. 292
[94] *Works*, I, pp. 306-7
[95] *Works*, I, p. 304

threatens destruction to our freedom, and with this certain and firm conviction in our hearts, to battle against this Power, to offer up our entire freedom, and thus to perish."[96]

The problem of the relation of freedom to selfhood or self-consciousness, so important in the *Inquiries,* is expounded in the *Letters.* "Where there is absolute freedom there is absolute blessedness and vice versa. But no self-consciousness is any longer conceivable in conjunction with absolute freedom."[97] The distinction between Freedom and Necessity, though insisted upon, is found, in the *Letters,* to disappear in a "higher unity." "Whoever has reflected upon Freedom and Necessity, found for himself that in the Absolute these principles must be *united.* The Absolute acts with freedom because it acts only through its own unconditioned power, with necessity because only thus can it act in accord with its essence, according to the inner necessity of its being. In it there is no longer a Will which could depart from Law, but also no Law which the Absolute did not give through its own acts, no Law which would have reality independent of its activities. Absolute Freedom and absolute Necessity are identical."[98] And here in a footnote, he links his thought with Spinoza's, as in the *Inquiries,* and defends Spinoza against the charge of having denied God's Freedom.

A shift from the conception of Freedom as an axiomatic and structural principle to the conception of Freedom as what may be called a principle of explanation, is made in the years 1796-1797.[99] Taking a sense of Freedom as a matter of common consciousness, he seeks to explain the

[96] *Works,* I, p. 336
[97] *Works,* I, p. 324
[98] *Works,* I, pp. 330-1
[99] *Works,* I, pp. 343-452

reality of the possibility of choice among alternatives; the absence of complete determinism in a world governed by law being, in his view, explicable only in terms of this immediate sense of freedom.[100] In the concept of Freedom we have "what Archimedes sought but did not find, a fulcrum on which reason can rest its lever, without therefore placing it in the present or in a future world but only in the *inner sense of freedom,* because it unites both worlds in itself and must also be the principle of explanation for both."[101] The words "inner sense of freedom" are, as Schelling mentions in a footnote, Kant's phrase in his tract *On the Genteel Tone in Philosophy.*

Not only as a principle of explanation but also as a principle of action Schelling invokes the idea of Freedom, recalling the conviction, quoted above, that "man is born to act and not to speculate."[102] The emphasis upon activity is recurrent, whether with reference to the activity of man or of nature. "To treat nature philosophically means to lift it out of the dead mechanism in which it appears to be imprisoned, to vitalize it, as it were, with Freedom, and to transport it into its own free development. This means, in other words, to disentangle oneself from the common view, which regards nature only as what happens, at most activity as a result, not the activity itself in action."[103]

But human action, activity, implies limitation, however much it evidences freedom. "Thus that I choose precisely C among various objects, B, C, D, must in its ultimate basis lie in me myself. But this basis can indeed not reside in my Freedom, for it is only through this limitation of my free

[100] *Works,* I, p. 439
[101] *Works,* I, p. 401
[102] *Works,* I, p. 243
[103] *Works,* I, p. 13

activity in the direction of a specific object that I become conscious of myself, and free. Withal, before I am free, that is conscious of freedom, my freedom must already be limited and certain free actions must be made impossible for me even before I am free."[104] In the external world, changes which take place through free activity appear as the products of law and "as if Freedom had no part at all in their production."[105] With respect to the individual the question is not "whether the ego is absolute, but whether it is free insofar as it is not absolute, insofar as it is empirical. Now it is just in our solution that it is evident that the will may be called free in a transcendental sense only insofar as it is, or appears to be, empirical. For Will, insofar as it is absolute, is itself exalted above Freedom, and far from being subject to any law, is itself the source of all law. But insofar as absolute will makes its appearance, it can only make its appearance through arbitrariness, in order to appear as absolute . . . But only this appearance of absolute will is really Freedom, or what is commonly understood as Freedom."[106]

The conviction that genuinely free activity is action through inner necessity, appears early in Schelling's writings: "Free self-determination is thus a contradiction because in absolutely free activity the conditioned factor and the conditioning factor are not two different factors, but one and the same, like the essence of the circle and the condition due to which all points of the circumference are equally distant from the center . . . Free activity or, as this term is redundant, *activity* in itself, is thus only genuine when the consequences of a thing are the results of its

[104] *Works,* III, p. 549
[105] *Works,* III, p. 566
[106] *Works,* III, p. 551

essential being, due to the Law of Identity. From this we can then gain the insight that all other Freedom, save that which is in Divinity, is naught, and that only God can be called truly free. For God's activity is God's essence and vice versa, and nothing can be a product of God which is not the result of the simple idea of his Being and is like to it."[107] The "theosophical" note of Schelling's later work, including the *Inquiries,* is surely discernible in the above lines as in the following sentences from the same work: "He whose actions are good and free is unable, to be sure, to act independently, and it is God who acts in him. But the good deed is not done without his knowledge. It is the consequence of Divinity in that it is the essence of *his* soul, and thus accords with the adequate idea which he has of it so that he alone is truly free in his activity."[108]

This motif, a *Leitmotif* indeed, of the relation of individual freedom to God, appears again and again. "In the soul (of the individual) as such, there is no Freedom, for only the Divine is truly free, and the essence of the soul insofar as it is divine."[109] . . . "Intimately connected with the concept of individual freedom are the concepts of evil, sin, guilt, punishment, etc."[110] And again: "To know that it is not we who act, but that a divine necessity acts in us, gives us peace and elevates us forever above all empty longing, fear and hope. This carries us to our goal and nothing derived from absolute Freedom can stand in conflict with it, for it itself is this absolute Freedom."[111]

Here we come to the problem of the relation of necessity and freedom in God. "In God there is the absolute har-

[107] *Works,* VI, p. 539
[108] *Works,* VI, p. 551
[109] *Works,* VI, p. 541
[110] *Works,* VI, p. 542
[111] *Works,* VI, p. 554

mony of Necessity and Freedom. God is absolutely free, for all is the consequence of the idea of his Being, without any conditioning factor within him or outside him. God is not influenced by a command, by a purpose, by a good which he imposes upon himself. He is absolutely good due to the nature of his being. God's action is therefore absolutely free as it is absolutely necessary."[112]

Reverting to the problem of man's inherent tendency to sin, intimated in the quotation above,[113] Schelling asserts that "philosophers, priests, and poets have ascribed to man an original tendency to Evil which is, in a certain sense, really undeniable. Only, in view of the usual presentations of this tendency, the remarkable thing is that it is supposed to be a tendency capable of moral responsibility. But that which precedes all specific acts is nothing else than Freedom, even in the sense of our moralists. It is the tendency to be absolute in oneself, the assumed power to be able to act autonomously and independently. Thus, original evil consists precisely in man's desire to be something independent and autonomous. From this it is easily deduced that morality which is derived from this very independent and autonomous activity may indeed in specific instances, conflict with the Right and the Good, but in principle and basically is in entire agreement with it."[114]

Interests supposedly characteristic of Schelling's later years, "theosophical" and "mythological" concerns, appear at least as early as the essay on *Philosophy and Religion* of the year 1804.[115] In this work Schelling declares that Divine Revelation required the falling away from the

[112] *Works,* VI, p. 553; cf. also p. 565
[113] *Works,* VI, p.542
[114] *Works,* VI, p. 561
[115] *Works,* VI, pp. 11-70

Absolute of finite and corporeal beings. He holds it to be "distinctively characteristic of Absoluteness that it endows its counterpart with its own Being and also with independence. This being-in-itself, this true and genuine reality of the primal object of vision, is Freedom. That which reappears as Freedom in the world of phenomena, follows from that primal independence of the counterpart, and is the final trace and, as it were, the seal of Divinity in the world which has fallen away (from the Absolute) . . . The counterpart is absolute and free only in absolute necessity. Hence insofar as it is separated from necessity in its *own* attribute, as being free, it ceases to be free itself and becomes entwined with that necessity which is the negation of that absoluteness, and thus purely finite . . . The basis of the possibility of a fall lies in Freedom."[116]

"This relationship of possibility and actuality is the basis of the appearance of Freedom, which is indeed inexplicable since its very conception consists in its being conditioned only by itself. But its primary source, whence it flows into the world of phenomena, can and must be explicated . . . As Freedom is witness to the primal absoluteness of Things, but just on that account is also the recurring possibility of a Fall, so empirical necessity is nothing but the fallen aspect of Freedom, the compulsion into which it turns by reason of its separation from its primal Form . . . On the other hand, the soul, in identity with the Primordial lifts itself above that necessity which opposes Freedom, to that necessity which is absolute Freedom itself. Therein Reality, which appears independent of Freedom in the course of Nature, is brought into harmony with it."[117] . . . "If the soul in its initial finitude has a relation to Freedom and is

[116] *Works,* VI, pp. 39-40
[117] *Works,* VI, pp. 52-3

a result of selfhood, then every subsequent condition of the soul, down to the present, can only stand in this relationship. Thus the necessary concept through which alone the present is tied to the future, is the concept of guilt or of innocence."[118]

In the course of history, however, finitude and corporeality will be brought back to the Absolute. "For since God is the absolute harmony of Necessity and Freedom, which can, however, only be expressed in totality and not in differentiated instances in history, so history itself is but a sequential and developmental revelation of God . . . History is an epic composed in God's spirit. Its two chief parts are, first, the departure of humanity from its center to the greatest distance therefrom; and, second, its return. The former is, as it were, the Iliad, the latter the Odyssey of history. In the former the direction was centrifugal, in the latter it becomes centripetal. The great purpose of the total world scene expresses itself in this way in history. Ideas, spirits, had to fall from their center, had to enter nature, the general realm of the fall, in differentiation, in order that they might later return as differentiated to the realm of Indifference and, reconciled to it, remain in it without disturbing it."[119]

The posthumously published lectures delivered privately to a congenial group of friends in Stuttgart in 1810,[120] and thus belonging to the very year following the publication of the *Inquiries,* contain numerous repetitions of thoughts presented in this work.[121] Schelling must inevitably have had his own work in mind in contrast to other defenses

[118] *Works,* VI, p. 61
[119] *Works,* VI, p. 57
[120] *Works,* VII, pp. 417-484
[121] *Cf.* below, notes to pp. 363, 366, 373 and 415 (marginal pagination corresponding to *Works,* VII).

of Freedom when he said: "The defenders of Freedom usually only think of showing the independence of man from nature, which is indeed easy. But they leave alone man's inner independence from God, his freedom even with respect to God, because this is the most difficult problem.

"Thus since man occupies a middle place between the non-being of nature and the absolute Being, God, he is free from both. He is free from God through having an independent root in nature; free from nature through the fact that the divine is awakened in him, that which in the midst of nature is above nature. One may call the former, man's own (natural) aspect through which he is an individual, a personal being; the latter may be called his divine aspect. He is free, in the human sense, through being placed at the point of Indifference."[122]

In Schelling's final work, the *Philosophy of Revelation,*[123] the interest in freedom may seem subordinate, yet when he touches on this theme, it is with characteristic enthusiasm. Thus he writes, "We can recognize this world in which we find ourselves only as one outside divinity, indeed we must ever demand that it become *comprehensible* to us as a world outside divinity. The sense of our freedom requires this, which is satisfied only by a free relationship to God. This is a relationship which could not be one of inclusion . . . Ours is a feeling of freedom not only from God but also of freedom from this world from which there would be no deliverance if it were the divine world, for every effort to free ourselves from the world (were it divine) and to make ourselves independent, would be madness. For good or ill we would have to remain *in* the world and

[122] *Works,* VII, p. 458
[123] *Works,* 2nd series, III and IV

of the world in which we are, if there were no other, no divine world besides the present, towards which we strive and in which we can take part."[124] And this final tribute to Freedom recalls the encomium of Freedom as the "beginning and end of all philosophy,"[125] words written in 1795. "Freedom is our All-high, our Godhead, which we desire as the Final Cause of all things. We do not even desire perfect spirit if we cannot at the same time attain it as absolutely free spirit. Or rather, perfect spirit is for us only spirit which is also absolutely free."[126]

V

The "first scientific presentation" of the "living whole of philosophy"[127] Schelling believed himself to have given in his *Philosophy of Nature.* He does not however "deny that this correct view was long since present in individual minds. Indeed it was these very individuals who sought out the vital basis of nature, without fear of those terms of reproach—materialism, pantheism, etc.—which have ever been current against all genuine philosophy, and who were Natural Philosophers (in both senses of the term) in distinction from those dogmatists and abstract idealists who banished them as mystics."[128]

What, then, was Schelling's attitude towards and relationship to these "mystics?" Remembering his own sharp and cutting references to persons who substitute an employ-

[124] *Works,* 2nd series, III, pp. 353-4
[125] *Works,* I, p. 177
[126] *Works,* 2nd series, III
[127] *Works,* VII, p. 356
[128] *Works,* VII, p. 357

ment of labels for an understanding of ideas,[129] one may well hesitate to use so general a term as "mysticism" to describe his own attitude. Yet this choice of the term "Natural Philosophers" to designate these predecessors, inevitably links them to him, and his attitude is further revealed by tracing his interest in the work of these men, and especially Jacob Böhme, the shoemaker of Görlitz, from whose speculations on evil, original sin and free-will Schelling seems to have derived his conception of a "dark, negative principle" so important in the pages which follow.

Apparently it was the poet Ludwig Tieck who, in 1799, first brought Böhme's writings to the attention of Schelling, as well as of Novalis and Schlegel, when he visited the last named at Jena and arranged with him for the publication of a poem on Böhme in the *Athenäum*.[130] Plitt notes that Tieck as "inspired panegyrist" of Böhme had difficulty in persuading many, and that Fichte especially rejected the "enthusiast" as a "muddle-headed dreamer," but that Schelling showed himself receptive to Böhme's ideas.[131] Plitt points out that there was evidence that Schelling "already knew the writings of the theosophist in part" even if "he did not study them in detail," in a passage written in 1806: "I am not ashamed of the designation of many so-called enthusiasts, but will even accept it emphatically and boast of having learned from them . . . as soon as I can make the boast. My ideas and views were labelled by these terms even when I knew only their names. These accusations I will now seek to make valid. If, up to now, I have not seriously studied their writings, this has not been at all due to contempt, but to carelessness which should be reproved, and

[129] *Cf. Works,* VII, pp. 333-6 and pp. 338, 344, 372, 410
[130] Kophe, *Ludwig Tieck,* I, p. 252
[131] *Letters,* I, pp. 246-7

of which, in the future, I will no longer allow myself to be guilty."[132]

In any case, in 1802 he had written to Berlin, to August Wilhelm Schlegel, asking him to try to buy him the quarto edition of Böhme,[133] and in 1804 he apparently received a "glorious edition of J. B." from his friend Windischmann.[134] Reference to this again appears in a letter written in 1809 to his friend Schubert, asking him to look for the quarto edition of Böhme "at any price" since he—Schelling—had given his to Franz Baader who had "so long pined for it."[135] It was indeed Baader[136] "a very learned man and great lover of mystical and theosophical writings,"[137] "a glorious prophet and splendid human being,"[138] who, as indicated in the *Inquiries,* stimulated Schelling's reflections on the nature of evil. According to Baader, Jacob Böhme was the only one who recognized "that Evil in itself was nothing but the fixed striving of a creature, a striving deep-rooted and Tantalus-like, not towards its creator but altogether for itself and thus to be and to live in itself."[139]

In his *History of Modern Philosophy* Schelling wrote of Böhme as being "the most remarkable individual" among the theosophists: "One must distinguish Jacob Böhme in whose work all is of the purest and most original nature from another class of mystics in whose work there is nothing living and original but where everything is already corrupted. In this class there belongs especially the well known St. Martin. In him one no longer hears, as in

[132] *Works,* VII, p. 120
[133] *Letters,* I, p. 376
[134] *Letters,* II, p. 10
[135] *Letters,* II, p. 162
[136] *Cf. Works,* VII, pp. 366, 373, 414
[137] *Letters,* II, p. 101
[138] *Letters,* II, p. 109
[139] *Baaders Sämmtliche Werke,* XIII, p. 176

Böhme, the original inspiration, but only the copyist or recorder of another's ideas, which are moreover prepared for purposes of another kind. That which is still living in Böhme is dead in St. Martin, only the cadaver still remains, as it were, the embalmed corpse, the mummy of one who once lived, as it is presented in secret societies which pursue their interests in alchemy, magic, and theurgic practises."[140]

And in his final work Schelling wrote: "One cannot avoid saying of Böhme that he is a miracle in the history of humanity and especially in the history of the German mind. If one could ever forget what a treasure of natural profundity of mind and heart is to be found in the German nation, one would only have to remind oneself of Böhme. He is, in his way, just as far exalted above the ordinary psychology by which one seeks to explain him and is as little explicable by it as is mythology. As the mythologies and theogonies of primitive peoples anticipated science, so Böhme anticipated all scientific systems of modern philosophy in his description of the birth of God. Jacob Böhme was born in 1575, René Descartes in 1596. What was intuition and the immediate inspiration of nature in Böhme appears in Spinoza, who died one hundred years after Böhme was born, as developed rationalism. But in the course of this development the great insight into Nature found in Böhme, was completely driven out of philosophy. For Spinoza's physics is in no way to be distinguished from the purely mechanistic and soulless physics of Descartes. Böhme is really a theogonic personality, but it was just this which prevented him from raising himself to free world-creation and just thereby to the freedom of positive philosophy. As is well known Böhme often speaks of the Wheel of

[140] *Works,* X, p. 190

Nature or of Birth. This is one of his most profound insights through which he expresses the dualism of forces in Nature laboring with itself, striving to bring itself to birth, but unable to do so. But it is just he himself who really is this Wheel, he who himself desires to give birth to this science but is unable to do so . . . This circular motion of his spirit shows itself outwardly in the fact that in each of his writings Böhme again starts from the outset, again sets forth the often and sufficiently explained beginnings without ever moving ahead or getting to new ground. In these beginnings he is always admirable, a true spectacle of Nature laboring with itself and yearning for freedom and autonomy but always remaining at the same spot, rotating about itself, unable to transform its rotation into real motion. Whenever Böhme goes beyond the beginnings of nature and into concrete matters, one becomes unable to follow him. Here every track is lost and it will ever remain a vain endeavor to translate him from the confused terms of his views into clarity, even if one employs, one after another, the concepts of Kant, Fichte, the Philosophy of Nature and finally even Hegel."[141]

In the earlier work Schelling discusses, in further detail, his estimate of theosophical philosophy and of the relations of theosophy, mysticism, and philosophy.[142] According to Schelling, those people should be called theosophists, and not philosophers "who do not call themselves believers-on-the-basis-of-reason but who place themselves on an equal footing with those who are and declare themselves to be directly inspired by God."[143] . . . "As this vision cannot be

[141] *Works,* 2nd division, III, pp. 123-4

[142] *Works,* X, pp. 184-192. Hubert Beckers, in an address commemorating the centenary of Schelling's birth, called attention to these significant passages here translated *in extenso.*

[143] *Works,* X, p. 184

communicated and as it is thus something secret and mystical, theosophy is, insofar, a type of mysticism. There is (1) a merely practical or subjective mysticism which makes no claims to being science. But there is also (2) an objective mysticism, which makes claims to objective knowledge. This is theosophy, which is theoretic or speculative mysticism, and though it does not assume scientific (rational) form, nevertheless makes claims to speculative content."[144]

"The utterances of theoretic mystics are indeed to a great extent incomprehensible, and we do not behold them in the blessed calm in which those must be thought to persist who are really enraptured, but in a mighty struggle, exhausting themselves in a great battle; their utterances are of such a compulsive kind that we are obliged to think of them as involved in a process. If they were really in the center they would needs be silent. But they wish to talk at the same time, to express themselves, and to express themselves for the sake of those who are outside the center. Therein lies the self-contradiction of theosophy."[145]

"I speak of those who are theosophists genuinely, originally and through a true peculiarity of their nature; not of those who go out, as it were, as knights errant on an intellectual adventure or affect to be theosophists in order to give themselves the appearance of profound insight, and because they believe that they can thus more easily and quickly excite attention than by honest, scientific work. Theosophy is altogether at odds with the constitution of the present life; the theosophist denies himself the greatest advantage of the present condition, distinct, discriminating knowledge which takes apart and keeps apart all things,

[144] *Works,* X, p. 185
[145] *Works,* X, p. 187

which is, to be sure, also a transition, but in the sense that the whole present life is a transition."[146]

"Thus there is here the boundary between theosophy and philosophy which he who loves science will chastely seek to preserve without permitting himself to be led astray by the apparent wealth of material to be found in the theosophical systems."[147]

"Nowadays the conception of mysticism, of mystics, is used by ignorant persons in the strangest way, when, for instance they immediately call anyone a mystic who believes in a revelation, even though he believes in this in the most historic sense . . . The simple conception of mystical, which many have made for themselves, is as follows: Everything which transcends my individual powers of comprehension I will call mystical—even presuming it were a sentence which had been established by purely scientific and altogether methodical development, for there must simply be nothing which transcends our powers of comprehension, nor should someone claim to have attained what we have declared once and for all unattainable."[148]

"In fact that which is preeminently mystical is Nature itself, and that in Nature which is most material, and that which those enemies of all mysticism perhaps regard as least mystical, for instance their appetite for good food and drink—sensation as such and the operation of the senses, these are surely the most hidden of all things that occur in Nature."[149]

"Nevertheless mysticism has always been distinguished in contrast with rationalism. Thus no one is a mystic by

[146] *Works,* X, p. 188
[147] *Works,* X, p. 189; *cf. Works,* VIII, p. 204
[148] *Works,* X, pp. 190-1
[149] *Works,* X, p. 191

reason of that which he asserts, but by the manner in which he asserts it. Mysticism only expresses the contrast with formal, scientific knowledge. No assertion is to be called mystical solely because of its content, no matter how it may have been arrived at, even though its content may agree with the assertion of some mystic. For if one were never to assert anything which a mystic had at some time or other also asserted, one would in the end be unable to assert anything. - Only that tendency of the mind can be called mysticism, which scorns all scientific foundation or analysis and wishes to derive all true knowledge from a so-called inner Light, which indeed does not shine for all but is shut away in the individual, from an immediate revelation, from a merely ecstatic intuition or mere emotion . . . The same truth can thus be mystical for one which is scientific for another and vice versa. For it is mystical for him who declares it on the basis of a merely subjective emotion or from an assumed revelation; it is scientific for him who declares it from the depths of science and who alone, therefore, truly understands it."[150]

That Schelling considered his own thought to be scientific can hardly be doubted, though it would be well to bear in mind the precise sense in which he used the term.[151] That he was sympathetic to "mysticism," the foregoing quotations make evident, and a reader of the *Inquiries into the Nature of Human Freedom*, as well as students of his other works, may well come to the conclusion that his sympathy at least at times introduced into his own writings elements of "mysticism" and, it may be, of "theosophy."

The question may then be raised whether the traditional interpretation of Schelling's thought solely as a stepping

[150] *Works*, X, pp. 191-2

[151] *Cf.* above, section II of this Introduction.

stone from Kant and Fichte to Hegel has not been a misreading of the history of modern philosophy and has not involved a misconception of Schelling's true place in the record of western thought. To read a writer largely as a transitional figure between two other, greater, men rather than for his own sake, is dangerous always. And in the case of Schelling, it may be asked whether this reading has not associated him too exclusively with one intellectual sequence, to the neglect of another. For it is to a philosophic tradition which has often passed as theology that he might also be linked, if one were mindful of the resemblance of the preoccupations and problems of Schelling's thought to those of Neo-Platonic Christianity in Patristic writings, in the Lutheran Reformation and in traditional Protestant mysticism.

F. W. J. SCHELLING'S

Philosophical Inquiries into

THE NATURE OF HUMAN FREEDOM

and matters connected therewith

1809

[Throughout the translation the *alphabetical* reference notations are to the translator's notes which will be found grouped together on pages 99-118. The *numerical* reference notations in the translation are those of Schelling's "Works," VII pp. 333-416, and refer to the notes at the foot of the page of the translation as of the original. The italicized numerals in the margins indicate the pages of the original, which pagination is also shown in subsequent German editions. All words in square brackets are by the translator.]

[a] FOREWORD[1]

THE AUTHOR finds but little to remark about the following treatise. 333[b]

Since reason, thought and knowledge are ordinarily accounted distinctive to the realm of spirit, the contrast of Nature and Spirit was at first readily taken up in these terms. This way of looking at the matter was adequately justified by the firm belief that reason is found only in man, the conviction that all thought and knowledge are completely subjective and that Nature altogether lacks reason and thought, and also by the universally prevalent mechanistic attitude,—even the dynamic factor which Kant revived having again passed over into a higher mechanism and being in no sense recognized in its identity with the spiritual. Now that the root of this old contrast has been dislodged, the implanting of a sounder insight may confidently be entrusted to the general progress towards better understanding.

The time has come for the higher distinction or, rather, for the real contrast, to be made manifest, the contrast between Necessity and Freedom, in which alone the innermost center of philosophy comes to view.

The author has limited himself entirely to investigations in the Philosophy of Nature, after a first general presenta-

[1] These remarks originally constituted a part of the Preface to *Schelling's Philosophical Writings. Volume I,* Landshut 1809, in which the treatise first appeared. Ed.

tion of his system (in *The Journal for Speculative Physics*)[c] the continuation of which was unfortunately interrupted by external circumstances. 334 | Following the beginning made in the essay on *Philosophy and Religion,* which indeed remained obscure because of faulty presentation, the present treatise is the first wherein the author offers with complete definiteness his conception of the part of philosophy which treats of the Ideal. Hence if the original presentation may be supposed to have had some importance, the present treatise should be placed alongside of it, since from the very nature of the subject the latter must contain deeper disclosures as to the entire system than all more fragmentary presentations.

Though the author has up to now nowhere expressed himself on the chief points discussed herein—on freedom of the will, good and evil, personality, etc. (with the single exception of the essay *Philosophy and Religion*), this has not prevented others from following their own pleasure and, apparently without regard to the content of that essay, from ascribing definite views to him even if these were altogether out of keeping with that work. Moreover self-constituted followers, so-called, seem to have brought forth, ostensibly in accordance with the fundamental principles of the author, a good many errors about these as well as other matters.

It would seem that only a finished and completed system could have followers in the true sense of the term.[a] Up to the present the author has never set up such a system, but has only presented special aspects of one and has very often shown these in certain relationships only, as, for instance, in polemical connections. Thus he explained his writings to be fragments of a whole, the connections between which it would require a more acute power of insight to recognize than self-constituted followers are apt to have, and more good will than one commonly finds among opponents. As the only scientific presentation of his system was not completed, its essential purport was understood by no one or by very few. Immediately upon the appearance of this fragment there began slander and misrepresentation on the one hand, and on the other, exposition, adaptation and transcription. Of all these the worst species of misrepresentation was the attempt at a supposedly more genial idiom, for at the same time a totally unrestrained poetic madness mastered people's heads. | Now it looks as though a healthier period were trying to emerge. Those things which are valid, productive and genuine are again being sought. The emptiness of those who have strutted about with sententious phrases of the new philosophy like French stage heroes or have been performing like tight-rope dancers, is beginning to be generally recognized for what it is. At the same time others who had been chanting the new tunes which they had picked up, in every market place as though to the accompaniment of a hurdy-gurdy, have aroused such general disgust, that they will soon no longer be able to find an audience; especially if otherwise not ill disposed critics will stop saying that every unintelligible rhapsody which assembles a few characteristic expressions of a well-known author, is composed in accordance with his fundamental principles. Let the critics rather treat all such writers as peculiarly original, which is, indeed, what they at bottom wish to be and is, in a certain sense, what very many are.[a]

335

May this treatise, then, serve to overcome many a prejudice on the one hand, and much free and easy gossip on the other.

Finally we wish that those who have attacked the author with prejudice, whether directly or indirectly, would now state their views just as frankly as he has done here. If complete mastery of one's subject makes possible its free artistic development, the artificial corkscrew twists of polemical writing cannot, after all, be the true form of philosophy. But even more do we hope that the spirit of a common purpose may increasingly take hold; and that the spirit of sectarianism which all too often rules over Germans shall not prevent the achievement of an understanding and insight for the complete development of which Germans have ever seemed destined and which was, perhaps, never nearer to them than now[b].

Munich, March 31, 1809.

PHILOSOPHICAL investigations into the nature of human freedom may, in part, concern themselves with the correct conception of the term; for though the feeling of freedom is ingrained in every individual, the fact itself is by no means so near to the surface that merely to express it in words would not require more than common clarity and depth of perception. In part such investigations may be concerned with the relation of this concept to a whole systematic world view. But here, as indeed everywhere, these two sides of the investigation coincide, since no conception can be defined in isolation and depends for its systematic completion on the demonstration of its connections with the whole. This is especially the case in the conception of freedom, for if it has any reality at all it cannot be a merely subordinate or incidental conception but must be one of the dominant central points of the system. To be sure, according to an ancient but by no means forgotten tradition, the idea of freedom is said to be entirely inconsistent with the idea of system, and every philosophy which makes claim to unity and completeness is said to end in denying freedom. It is not easy to dispute general affirmations of this sort; for who knows what restricting notions have already been attached to the word "system" itself, so that the assertion declares something which, to be sure, is very true but also very commonplace. Or if the opinion be advanced that the concept of freedom contradicts the concept of system altogether and inherently, then it is

337 extraordinary that | some sort of system must be present and coexist with freedom at least in the divine understanding. For individual freedom in some manner or other has a place in the universe, it matters not whether this be thought of realistically or idealistically. The general statement that this system [in the divine understanding][a] can never be revealed to human insight again means nothing at all. For it may be true or false according to how it is interpreted, depending on the definition of the principle by virtue of which man can in any wise attain knowledge. The assumption that such knowledge is possible may be characterized in the words of Sextus about Empedocles: the literally minded and the uninformed may imagine that the claim to have this knowledge arises from boastfulness and a sense of superiority towards others, qualities which should be foreign to anyone who has had even a slight training in philosophy. But whoever takes the theory of physics as his point of departure and knows that the doctrine 'like is recognized by like' is a very ancient one (supposed to come from Pythagoras but found in Plato and declared long before by Empedocles)—such a one will understand that the philosopher maintains the existence of this (divine) knowledge, because he alone comprehends the god outside himself through the god within himself by keeping his mind pure and unclouded by evil.[1] But, alas, those who are unsympathetic towards science, traditionally regard it as a kind of knowledge which is quite external[b] and lifeless like conventional geometry.

A simpler and more decisive course [in dealing with the whole problem][c] would be to deny that system exists even in the will or mind of the Primal Being, and to declare

[1] Sext. Empir. adv. Grammaticos. L, I, c. 13, p. 238 ed. Fabric.

that after all there are only individual wills each being a center for itself and, in Fichte's[d] phrase, each Ego being the absolute Substance. However, reason which strives towards unity, as well as the emotional assurance of freedom and personality, is ever denied only by an arbitrary assertion which prevails for a while but at last gives way. Thus Fichte's doctrine was obliged to bear testimony to | Unity even if only in the inadequate form of a moral order in the world; but by so doing it immediately fell into contradictions and untenable assertions. Much as may be adduced from a merely historic consideration of previous systems in support of the contention that freedom and systematic unity are incompatible, we have nowhere found arguments derived from the nature of reason and knowledge themselves. Hence it seems that the connection between the concept of freedom and a total world view will always remain the subject of an inevitable problem which, if it is not solved, will leave the concept of freedom ambiguous and philosophy, indeed, totally without value. For this great problem alone constitutes the unconscious and invisible mainspring of all striving for knowledge from the lowest to the highest. Without the contradiction of necessity and freedom not only philosophy but every nobler ambition of the spirit would sink to that death which is peculiar to those sciences in which that contradiction serves no function. To withdraw from the conflict by foreswearing reason looks more like flight than victory. Another person would have the same right to turn his back on freedom in order to throw himself into the arms of reason and necessity, without there being any cause for self-congratulation on either side. *338*

The same argument has been more pointedly expressed in the sentence: Pantheism is the only possible system of reason but is inevitably fatalism.[1] It cannot be denied that it is a splendid invention to be able to designate entire points of view at once with such general epithets. If one has once discovered the right label for a system, everything else follows of its own accord and one is spared the trouble of investigating its essential characteristics in greater detail. Even an ignorant person can | render judgment upon the most carefully thought out ideas as soon as they are presented to him with the help of such labels. But after all, in an extraordinary assertion of this kind everything depends upon the closer definition of the concept. For it cannot be denied that if pantheism meant nothing but the doctrine of the immanence of all things in God, every rational view would have to adhere to this teaching in some sense or other. But just in what sense is the crucial question here. That the fatalistic point of view can be combined with pantheism is undeniable; but that it is not essentially tied to it is made clear by the fact that many are driven to this pantheistic outlook precisely because of the liveliest sense of freedom. Most people, if they were honest, would have to admit that in terms of their ideas individual freedom seems to be in contradiction to almost all attributes of a Highest Being, omnipotence for instance. In maintaining freedom, a power which by its nature is unconditioned is asserted to exist alongside of and outside the divine power, which in terms of their ideas is inconceivable. As the sun outshines all the other celestial lights in the firmament, so, but to a greater degree, infinite power

339

[1] Earlier assertions of this sort are well known. We leave unanswered the question whether the declaration of Friedrich Schlegel may possibly have another meaning in his work, *On the Language and Wisdom of the Hindus,* page 141: "Pantheism is the system of pure reason."[a]

extinguishes all finite power. Absolute causal power in one being leaves nothing but unconditional passivity for all the rest. Thus there follows the dependence of all earthly creatures upon God, their very persistence being nothing but a constantly renewed creation in which the finite being is produced not as something generic and undetermined but as this particular individual with such and such thoughts, desires and actions and no others. To say that God restrains his omnipotence so that man can act, or that he permits freedom, explains nothing; for if God withdrew his power for an instant, man would cease to be. Since freedom is unthinkable in contradistinction to omnipotence, is there any other escape from this argument than by placing man and his freedom in the divine being, by saying that man exists not outside God but in God, and that man's activity itself belongs to God's life? From this very point of view mystics and religious temperaments in all ages have come to believe in the unity of man with God, a belief which seems to appeal to our inmost feelings as much as, | or even more than, it does to reason and speculation. Scripture itself finds precisely in the consciousness of freedom the seal and earnest of the faith that we live and have our being in God.[a] How can that very doctrine necessarily be in dispute with freedom which so many have asserted before mankind for the particular purpose of saving freedom?

340

Another interpretation of pantheism is, to be sure, one which is generally considered to be more to the point, namely that it constitutes a total identification of God with all things, a confusion of creature and creator, from which a mass of still more difficult and unsupportable assertions are then deduced. However a more complete differentiation of things and God can hardly be conceived than is made in the teaching of Spinoza[b] which is said to be the classic instance of that identification. God is that which is in itself and is conceived solely through itself; whereas the finite necessarily exists in another being and can only be conceived with reference to it. Manifestly, in consequence of this distinction, things are not different from God merely in degree or because of their limitations, as a superficial view of the doctrine of modes might indeed seem to imply, but they differ from God *toto genere.* Thus whatever their relation to God may be, they are absolutely differentiated from God through the fact that they can exist only in and dependent upon another being (namely himself), and that their concept is a derivative one which would not even be possible without the concept of God. By contrast, the concept of God alone is independent and primary and self-affirming, all else being related to it only as what is affirmed, or as the consequence to the antecedent. Only on this assumption are other attributes of things valid, their eternality for instance. God is by nature eternal; things are so only through him and as a consequence of his existence—that is, in a derivative manner. Just because of this difference, the sum of all individual things cannot constitute God, as is usually set forth, since no kind of combination can transform that which is by nature derived into that which is by nature original, just as little as all the points

341 in a circumference | taken together can constitute the whole, since the latter by its very definition necessarily precedes them. Still more preposterous is the inference that in Spinoza each individual being must be identified with God. For even if the daring expression that each object is a modified God were found in his work, the elements of this concept are so contradictory that it falls apart in the very act of being assembled. A modified God, that is to say a derived God, is not God in the real, distinctive sense;

this one addition puts things back in their place which everlastingly distinguishes them from God. The reason for such misinterpretations which other systems have also experienced in full measure, is found in the general misunderstanding of the law of identity[a] or of the meaning of the copula in judgment. It can readily be made comprehensible to a child that in no possible proposition, which is generally mistaken to declare the identity of subject and predicate, the equivalence of the two or even their immediate connection is affirmed. Thus, for example, the proposition, "This body is blue," does not mean that the body in and by reason of its being a body is also a blue body, but only that the object designated as this body is also blue though not in the same sense. Nevertheless, this mistake which indicates complete ignorance as to the nature of the copula, has repeatedly been made in our time with respect to the higher application of the law of identity. If, for example, the proposition is advanced that the Perfect is the Imperfect, it signifies: the Imperfect exists not by means of those attributes in and through which it is imperfect, but by means of the perfection which it contains. But for our contemporaries it has this significance: Perfection and Imperfection are equivalent, everything is one and the same, the worst and the best, folly and wisdom. Or take the proposition: the Good is the Evil—by which is meant: Evil has no power to exist in itself; that which is real in it, considered in itself, is good. This statement is held to mean: the eternal difference between right and wrong, between virtue and sin, is being denied, and from the point of view of logic they are the same. | Or if, in another connection, it is explained that necessity and freedom are one, meaning that in the last instance the essence of the moral world is also the essence of the world of nature, *342* it is taken to mean: Freedom is nothing but a force of nature, a mainspring which like all others is subordinate to mechanism. The same thing occurs with the proposition that the soul and body are one, which is made to mean: The soul is material, a gas, ether, nerve current and the like. For the opposite, that body is soul, or, in the preceding statement, that apparent necessity can itself be a case of freedom, though this could quite as well be deduced from the proposition, is shrewdly put to one side. Such misunderstandings, if they are not intentional, imply a degree of dialectical immaturity which Greek philosophy transcended almost in its first beginnings and make the recommendation of a thorough course in logic an urgent duty. The profound logic of the ancients distinguished subject and predicate as the antecedent and the consequent (*antecedens et consequens*) and thus expressed the real meaning of the law of identity. Even a tautological statement, if it is not to be altogether meaningless, retains this relationship. Thus if one says: A body is body; he is assuredly thinking something different in the subject of the sentence than in its predicate. In the former, that is, he refers to the unity, in the latter to the individual qualities contained in the concept, body, which are related to the unity as the *antecedens* to the *consequens.* Just this is the meaning of another older explanation, according to which subject and predicate are discriminated as being the unexpressed and the expressed (*implicitum et explicitum*).[1]

[1] Mr. Reinhold[a] wished to reconstruct the whole of philosophy by means of logic, though he does not seem to know what was already said by Leibniz—in whose footsteps he imagines himself to be walking—concerning the meaning of the copula, in connection with the objections of Wissowatius (Opp T. I ed. Dutens, p. 11).[b] Mr. Reinhold, too, is still laboring endlessly in this maze wherein he confuses identity with sameness. In a publication

| Nonetheless, the defenders of the foregoing assertion will now say, we are not at all concerned in pantheism with the fact that God is all (which cannot well be avoided in view of the usual conception of his attributes) but we are concerned with the circumstance that things are as 343

which lies before us there is the following passage which comes from him: "According to the dicta of Plato and Leibniz the task of philosophy consists in demonstrating the subordination of the finite to | the Infinite; according to Xenophanes, Bruno, Spinoza and Schelling it consists in showing the unconditioned unity of the two." Insofar as the above contrast implies that unity is here manifestly intended to signify sameness, I assure Mr. Reinhold that he is mistaken, at least with respect to the two last named. Where is a more pointed expression of the subordination of the Finite to the Infinite to be found than the one from Spinoza referred to above?[a] The living must defend against defamation those who are no longer present, as we expect those who will live after us to do in our behalf in the same event. I speak only of Spinoza, and ask what this procedure should be called which consists in shouting abroad whatever one wishes about systems of thought without knowing them thoroughly, as though it were a trifle to ascribe to them this or that product of one's imagination? In good society it would ordinarily be called *lack of conscience.*—According to another passage in the same publication, R. finds the basic error of all recent philosophy, as well as of certain earlier systems, in the failure to distinguish (the confusion, interchanging of) unity (identity) with system (nexus), as well as of variety (diversity) with difference. This is not the first occasion on which R. finds those errors in his opponents which he imported into them. This seems to be the way in which he employs the *medicina mentis* he needs; as there are said to be cases of highly suggestible persons who were cured by means of drugs which they let others take for them. For who makes this error of confusing what he calls "unity" (but what is really sameness) with system more certainly than R. himself with respect to recent and earlier philosophy, construing Spinoza's being-of-all-things-in-God to mean the assertion of their sameness, and constantly regarding non-differentiation (with respect to substance or essence) as being non-distinction (with respect to form or logical conception). If Spinoza is really to be understood as R. construes him, then the well known statement that the object and the idea of the object are one, would have to be understood to mean that we could, for example, conquer the enemy with the idea of an army instead of with an army, etc.—consequences which serious and reflective men will consider beneath them. 343n naught, that this system does away with all individuality. To be sure this new characterization seems to be in contradiction to the preceding one, for if all things are as naught, how is it possible to confuse God with them? | For in this case there would be nothing at all except pure, unclouded divinity. Or, if there is nothing beside God (not only *extra Deum* but also *praeter Deum*) how then can he be 'all things' except in name; so that the entire conception seems to dissolve and evaporate into nothing. In any case it seems questionable whether much is gained by resurrecting such general labels, for though they may occupy places of honor in the history of heresy, they seem to be much too clumsy as handles for the products of the spirit in connection with which, as in the most delicate phenomena of nature, subtle modifications cause fundamental changes. It might moreover be doubted whether the last mentioned characterization is applicable even to Spinoza. For if he recognizes nothing beside (*praeter*) Substance, except its mere modes, with which he identifies things, then this conception is indeed an altogether negative one, which expresses nothing essential or positive. It serves at first, in fact, merely to define the relation of things to God, not what they may be, considered in themselves. But the inadequacy of this definition does not imply that things contain nothing at all which is positive, even though they be of a derivative nature. The most drastic expression in Spinoza is probably the statement: The individual being is Substance itself viewed in one of its modes, that is, in one of its consequences. If we let infinite Substance $= A$, and infinite Substance regarded in one of its consequences $= A/a$; then that which is positive in A/a is, indeed, A. But it does not follow on this account that $A/a = A$, i.e. that infinite Substance regarded in its consequences is to be

344

considered exactly the same as infinite Substance as such. Or, in other words, it does not follow that A/a is not a distinctive and particular substance, even though it be a consequence of A. To be sure this is not set forth in Spinoza. However we are, in the first place, speaking of pantheism in general; so that the only question is, whether the view expressed is inherently incompatible with Spinozism. This can scarcely be asserted, since it has been admitted that Leibniz's monads, which are precisely the same as | 345 what is expressed in the above A/a, are not a decisive measure against Spinozism. Without an interpretative amendment of this sort some of Spinoza's utterances remain puzzling, for instance the statement that the essence of the human soul is a vital idea of God's which is declared to be eternal and not transitory. Thus, even if Substance were but temporarily present in its other modes, A/b, A/c . . ., it would be eternally present in that one mode, the human soul, = a. And in this way as A/a, it would everlastingly and in an eternal way be divorced from itself as A.

To proceed, if the denial of freedom, not of individuality, should now be declared to be the essential characteristic of pantheism, then a multitude of systems would come under this heading which are otherwise essentially differentiated from it. For the true conception of freedom was lacking in all modern systems, that of Leibniz as well as that of Spinoza, until the discovery of Idealism. And the sort of freedom which many among us have conceived, even those boasting of the liveliest sense thereof, a freedom, namely, consisting of the mere mastery of intelligence over senses and passions, could be deduced from Spinoza himself without difficulty, indeed quite easily and with superior decisiveness. Thus it seems that the denial or affirmation of freedom in general is based on something quite other than the acceptance or non-acceptance of pantheism, the immanence of things in God. For if, at the first glance, it seems that freedom, unable to maintain itself in opposition to God, is here submerged in identity, it may be said that this apparent result is merely the consequence of an imperfect and empty conception of the law of identity. This principle does not express a unity which, revolving in the indifferent circle of sameness, would get us nowhere and remain meaningless and lifeless. The unity of this law is of an intrinsically creative kind. In the relation of | subject to predicate itself, we have already pointed out the relation of ground and consequence; and the law of sufficient reason is therefore just as ultimate as the law of identity. The Eternal, as such, must, on this account, also be this ground, without mediation. That for which the Eternal is by its nature the ground, is, to this extent, dependent and, from the point of view of immanence, is also conceived in the Eternal. But dependence does not exclude autonomy or even freedom. Dependence does not determine the nature of the dependent, and merely declares that the dependent entity, whatever else it may be, can only be as a consequence of that upon which it is dependent; it does not declare what this dependent entity is or is not. Every organic individual, insofar as it has come into being, is dependent upon another organism with respect to its genesis but not at all with regard to its essential being. It is not incongruous, says Leibniz, that he who is God could at the same time be begotten, or contrariwise; it is no more contradictory than for one who is son of a man himself to be a man. On the contrary, it would indeed be contradictory if that which is dependent or consequent were not autonomous. There would be dependence without something being dependent,

346

a result without a resultant (*consequentia absque consequente*), and therefore no true result; that is, the whole conception would vitiate itself. The same thing is true of concepts being implied in others. A single organ, like the eye, is possible only in the organism as a whole; nevertheless it has a life of its own, indeed a kind of freedom, as is manifestly proved through those diseases to which it is subject. If that which is conceived in another could not have its own life, there would be a concept without a conception; that is, nothing would be conceived. We attain a much loftier point of view by regarding the divine Being itself, the very idea of which would be completely incompatible with a result which was not a living creation,—that is, the positing of something autonomous. God is not a God of the dead but of the living. It is incomprehensible that an all-perfect Being could rejoice in even the most perfect mechanism possible. No matter how one pictures to oneself the procession of creatures from God, it can never be a mechanical production, no mere construction or setting up, | in which the construct is naught in itself. Just as certainly, it cannot be an emanation in which that which has flowed forth remains the same as its source, thus lacking individuality and independence. The procession of things from God is God's self-revelation. But God can only reveal himself in creatures who resemble him, in free, self-activating beings for whose existence there is no reason save God, but who are as God is. He speaks, and they are there. Though all the world's creatures were but the thoughts of the divine mind, they would on this very account necessarily have life. Thus thoughts are doubtless born in the soul; but a thought once born is an independent power which works on in its own way, and which indeed grows so great in the human soul that it masters its own

347

mother and prevails over her. However, divine imagination, which is the cause of the differentiation of the world's beings, is unlike human imagination and never gives to its creations a merely ideal reality. The products of divine imagination must be independent beings, for wherein does the limitation of our imagination consist than precisely in our seeing things as dependent?[a] God beholds all things in themselves. Only the Eternal exists in itself, as Self-secured, Will, Freedom. The concept of a derivative absoluteness or divinity is so little a contradiction that it is actually the central concept of all philosophy. This sort of divinity characterizes nature. Immanence in God is so little a contradiction of freedom that freedom alone, and insofar as it is free, exists in God, whereas all that lacks freedom, and insofar as it lacks freedom, is necessarily outside God.

Though so general a demonstration is in itself insufficient for one who sees more deeply, it nonetheless clears up this much—that the denial of formal freedom is not necessarily connected with pantheism. We do not anticipate having Spinozism brought up in opposition to us. It requires no little audacity to declare that a system, however construed in the thought of any individual, is *the* System of Reason, κατ' ἐξοχὴν , eternal and unchanging. What is meant by Spinozism? Can it be the entire teaching as set forth in the man's writings, including, for instance, | his mechanistic physics? Or according to what principle is one to select and discriminate, here, where everything is supposed to be so full of extraordinary and unique consistency? It will always remain a striking circumstance in the history of German intellectual development, that at any time the assertion could be made: The system which merges (as it was understood) God with all things, creatures with the creator, and makes all subordinate to blind,

348

irrational necessity, is the only possible system of reason and the only one capable of being developed by pure reason. In order to comprehend this we must recall the dominant spirit of an earlier age. At that time all minds had fallen victim to the mechanistic trend of thought which attained the pinnacle of its nefariousness in French atheism. In Germany, too, one began to regard and expound this type of thought as the only true and genuine philosophy. Meanwhile, as the native German temperament could never assimilate the consequences of this view, there at first appeared that conflict of mind and heart which is so typical of philosophical literature in recent times.[a] One abhorred the consequences of this mode of thinking, without being able to free oneself from its cause or to rise to a better way. There was the wish to voice these consequences; and as the German spirit could grasp this mechanistic philosophy only in its (supposedly) highest expression, the terrible truth was uttered in this way: All philosophy, absolutely all, which is based on pure reason alone, is, or will become, Spinozism. All men were now warned of the abyss; it was clearly laid bare before all eyes. The only remedy which still seemed possible was seized; only that bold utterance could bring on the crisis; it alone could frighten Germans away from this ruinous philosophy and lead them back to the Heart, to inwardness of feeling and to faith. Nowadays, as this type of thought has long since ceased to be and the higher light of Idealism shines for us, this same declaration would neither be comprehensible to a like extent nor promise the same results.[1]

[1] In a review[a] of Fichte's recent writings, in the Heidelberg Annuals of Literature (vol. 1, no. 6, p. 139) Mr. Friedrich Schlegel gives Fichte the advice to devote himself exclusively to Spinoza in his polemical undertakings, as only in Spinoza is there

349n

349 | Here, then, once and for all our definite opinion about Spinozism! This system is not fatalism because it lets things be conceived in God; for as we have shown, pantheism does not make formal freedom, at least, impossible. Spinoza must then be a fatalist for another reason, entirely independent of this. The error of his system is by no means due to the fact that he posits all *things in God,* but to the fact that they are *things*—to the abstract conception of the world and its creatures, indeed of eternal Substance itself, which is also a thing for him. Thus his arguments against freedom are altogether deterministic, and in no wise pantheistic. He treats the will, too, as a thing, and then proves, very naturally, that in every case of its operation it must be determined by some other thing, which in turn is determined by another, and so forth endlessly. Hence the lifelessness of his system, the harshness of its form, the bareness of its concepts and expressions, the relentless austerity of its definitions; this admirably in accord with the abstract outlook. Thence also, quite consistently, his mechanistic view of nature. Or can one doubt that even a dynamic conception of nature must necessarily bring about an essential change in the basic views of Spinozism? If the doctrine that all things are conceived in God is the basis of the entire system, it must at least first be vitalized and severred from abstractness before it can become the

to be found a system of pantheism perfect in its form and consistency, which—in accordance with the utterance set forth above[b] —is, at the same time, the System of Pure Reason. This advice might, of course, yield certain advantages, but is strange in view of the fact that Mr. Fichte is doubtless of the opinion that he already refuted Spinozism, (qua Spinozism) in his Science of Knowledge, in which his opinion is altogether correct.—Or is it possible that idealism is not a product of reason; and are pantheism and Spinozism really alone to retain the supposedly sad honor of being systems of reason?

principle of a system of reason. How general and vague is the expression, that the eternal beings are modes or consequences | of God; what a chasm there is here, needing to be filled in; what questions remain to be answered! Spinozism in its rigidity could be regarded like Pygmalion's statue, needing to be given a soul through the warm breath of love: but this comparison is imperfect, as Spinozism more closely resembles a work of art which has been sketched only in its most general outlines and in which, if it were endowed with a soul, one would still notice how many features were lacking or incompleted. It could more readily be compared to the most ancient likenesses of the divinities, which seemed all the more mysterious the fewer the features of individual lifelikeness apparent in them. In a word, it is a onesidedly realistic system, and although this expression sounds less damning than 'pantheism,' it nevertheless describes the peculiar nature of this system far more correctly, and is, moreover, not now used for the first time. It would be tedious to repeat the many explanations concerning this point which are to be found in the author's earliest writings. The expressed intention of his efforts was a mutual interpenetration of realism and idealism. Spinoza's fundamental concept, spiritualized by the principle of idealism (and changed at one essential point) was given a vital basis through the more elevated way of regarding nature, and through the recognized unity of what is dynamic with what is spiritual and emotional. From this there developed a Philosophy of Nature, which as a mere physics could indeed stand by itself, but which was always regarded, with respect to the whole of philosophy, as merely one of its parts (that is, its real part) and which would permit of being raised into a genuine system of reason only by first being completed by an ideal part

350

wherein freedom is sovereign. In this freedom, it was declared, the final intensifying[a] act was to be found through which the whole of nature found its transfiguration in feeling, in intelligence, and, ultimately, in will.—In the final and highest instance there is no other Being than Will. Will is primordial Being, and all predicates apply to it alone—groundlessness, eternity, independence of time, self-affirmation! All philosophy strives only to find this highest expression.

It is to this point that Idealism has raised philosophy, up to our time; | and only at this point are we really able to take up the investigation of our subject, since it could by no means be our purpose to take account of all those difficulties which can be raised (and have already been raised) against the concept of freedom on the basis of the one-sidedly realistic or dogmatic system. However, high as we have been placed in this respect by Idealism, and certain as it is that we owe to it the first formally perfect concept of freedom, Idealism itself is, after all, nothing less than a finished system. And as soon as we seek to enter into the doctrine of freedom in greater detail and exactitude, it nonetheless leaves us helpless. As regards systematic completeness, we observe that in an idealism which had been formulated into a system, it would by no means suffice to declare that "Activity, life and freedom are alone true reality." For even Fichte's idealism, subjective idealism, (which does not understand itself)[a] can go this far. Rather it is required that the reverse be proved too—that all reality (nature, the world of things) is based upon activity, life and freedom, or—in the Fichtean expression—that not only is the Ego all, but contrariwise too, all is Ego. The thought of making freedom the sum and substance of philosophy has eman-

351

cipated the human spirit in all its relationships, and not only with respect to itself and has given to science in all its parts a more powerful reorientation than any earlier revolution.[b] The idealistic conception is the true initiation into higher philosophy in our time and especially into a higher realism.[c] If only those who sit in judgment on this realism, or appropriate it, would reflect that freedom is its most essential presupposition, in what a different light would they then regard and comprehend it! Only he who has tasted freedom can feel the desire to make over everything in its image, to spread it throughout the whole universe. Whoever does not approach philosophy in this way, merely follows others and copies what they do without feeling why they do it. But it will always remain strange that Kant, after first distinguishing the things-in-themselves from | appearances only negatively, as being independent of time, and later, in the metaphysical explications of his *Critique of Practical Reason,* treated independence-of-time and freedom as correlative concepts, did not proceed to the thought of transferring this only possible positive conception of *per-se-ity* to things. By doing this he would immediately have raised himself to a higher standpoint, above the negativity which is characteristic of his theoretical philosophy. But, on the other hand, if freedom is the positive conception of *per-se-ity* as such, then the investigation of human freedom is again thrown back into generality, since intelligibility, upon which freedom alone was based, is then also the essence of things-in-themselves. Mere idealism is therefore not adequate to show the specific differentia, i.e. the precise distinctiveness of human freedom. Similarly it would be a mistake to believe that pantheism has been put aside and destroyed by idealism; an opinion which could only issue from confusing it with

352

one-sided realism. For it is immaterial to pantheism, as such, whether many individual things are conceived in an absolute Substance or many individual wills are conceived in one Primal Will. In the first case it would be realistic, in the second, idealistic; but its fundamental concept remains the same. From this very fact it can be seen in advance, that the most profound difficulties which lie in the concept of freedom will be as little solvable through idealism, taken in itself, as through any other incomplete system. For idealism supplies only the most general conception of freedom, and a merely formal one. But the real and vital conception of freedom is that it is a possibility of good and evil.

This is the point of profoundest difficulty in the whole doctrine of freedom, which has always been felt and which applies not only to this or that system, but, more or less, 353 to all:[1] | To be sure it applies most strikingly to the concept of immanence, for either real evil is admitted, in which case it is unavoidable to include evil itself in infinite Substance or in the Primal Will, and thus totally disrupt the conception of an all-perfect Being; or the reality of evil must in some way or other be denied, in which case the real conception of freedom disappears at the same time. But the difficulty is no slighter if even the faintest connection is assumed between God and the world order. For even if this is limited to a mere *concursus,* so-called, or to that necessary cooperation of God in the activity of his creatures (which must be assumed

[1] Mr. Friedrich Schlegel has the credit of having made this difficulty count especially against pantheism, in his essay on India and in numerous places; and it is only to be regretted in this connec- 353n tion, that this discerning scholar did not think it well to communicate his own views on the origin of evil and its relation to the good.

because of the essential dependence of the latter upon God, even if freedom is otherwise asserted) then God undeniably appears as co-author of evil. For permitting an entirely dependent being to do evil is, after all, not much better than cooperating with it in causing evil. Or, again, the reality of evil must be denied in some way or other. The proposition that all that is positive in creatures comes from God, must be asserted in this system too. Now if it is assumed that there is something positive in evil, then this positive [element] also comes from God. It may be objected to this, that what is positive in evil, insofar as it is positive, is good. Evil does not disappear in this way, any more than it is explained. For if that element in evil which has *being* is good, whence, then, comes that *wherein* it has its being, the *basis* which really constitutes the evil? An assertion quite different from the foregoing (though often, and recently, confused with it) is the statement that in evil there is nothing at all positive, or—otherwise expressed—that evil does not exist at all (not even in connection with or through something else which is positive) but that all actions are more or less positive, and that the difference between them is a mere plus or minus of perfection. In this view no antithesis is established, and all evil disappears entirely. | This would be the second possible position with regard to the statement that everything positive has its source in God. Then the power manifest in evil would indeed be relatively less perfect than the power in goodness, but in itself or without regard to this comparison it would itself be perfect and, like all perfection, would thus have to be derived from God. That which we call evil is only a lesser degree of perfection, which seems a defect only in our comparison but is none in nature. It cannot be denied that this is Spinoza's real

354

opinion. Someone might try to escape from this dilemma by answering: That which is positive, derived from God, is freedom, which in itself is indifferent to good and evil. However if he does not think of this indifference[a] in a merely negative way but as a vital, positive power for good and evil, then it cannot be understood how a power for evil can come from God who is regarded as utter goodness. As may be said in passing, it becomes clear in this connection, that if freedom really is what it must be in consequence of this conception (and it undoubtedly is) then the above attempt to deduce freedom from God is probably not correct either. For if freedom is a power for evil it must have a root independent of God. Compelled by this argument one may be tempted to throw oneself into the arms of dualism. However if this system is really thought of as the doctrine of two absolutely different and mutually independent principles, it is only a system of self-destruction and the despair of reason. But if the radical principle of evil is thought of as in any sense dependent on the good, then the whole difficulty of the derivation of evil from goodness is, to be sure, concentrated on a single Being, but the difficulty is rather increased than diminished in this way. Even if it is assumed that this second Being, as originally created, was good and fell from primal being through its own fault, the initial power to perform a deed in opposition to God still remains inexplicable in all systems of thought up to the present. Thus finally, | even if one wished to eliminate every connection between the world's creatures and God, and not merely to deny their identity, and if one wished to regard their present existence and thus the existence of the world as a withdrawal from God, the difficulty would only be pushed back a point but would not

355

be eliminated. For in order to have flowed forth from God, things must already have been in God in some way or other. And the doctrine of emanation could thus least of all be contrasted with pantheism, as it presupposes an original existence of things in God, obviously implying pantheism. To explain this withdrawal only the following could be maintained: Either the withdrawal is involuntary on the part of things, but not on the part of God, in which case they have been banished by God to a state of infelicity and wickedness, and God is thus the author of this condition; or it is involuntary on the part of both, caused perhaps by an excess of being, as some have expressed it—an altogether untenable conception; or it is deliberate on the part of things, a secession from God, the consequence, then, of a guilt which results in ever deeper degradation—in which case this original guilt is itself the evil and thus does not explain the origin of evil. But without this auxiliary thought, which if it explains the evil in the world thereby utterly extinguishes all the good and introduces pandaemonism instead of pantheism, every real distinction between good and evil disappears, in that very system of emanationism. The first principle is lost in the innumerable intermediary steps, and through gradual weakening becomes something that no longer has any semblance of goodness, approximately as Plotinos[1] cleverly but inadequately describes the transition of what was originally the Good into matter and evil. Thus through constant subordination and withdrawal there finally issues that from which nothing more can come, and just this, which is incapable of further production, is evil. Or, if there is anything besides primal Being then there must

[1] Ennead I, L. viii, c. 8.

also be a last and least Being which no longer has anything of the primal in its make-up, and this is matter and the necessity of evil.

356 | In view of these considerations it does not seem quite justifiable to throw the whole burden of those difficulties on a single system, especially as so little satisfaction is yielded by the supposedly higher system which is contrasted with it. The generalities of idealism can provide no help here either. Nothing can be achieved at all by such attenuated conceptions of God as *actus purissimus* and similar notions which earlier philosophy set forth, or by such concepts as the newer thought constantly produces in its concern to separate God as far as possible from all of nature. God is more of a reality than is a mere moral world-order, and he has in him quite other and more vital activating powers than the barren subtlety of abstract idealists ascribes to him. The abhorrence of all reality which might sully the spiritual through any contact with it, must naturally blind the eye to the origin of evil too. Idealism, if it is not grounded in a vital realism will become just as empty and attenuated a system as the Leibnizian, Spinozistic or any other dogmatic philosophy. The whole of modern European philosophy since its inception (through Descartes) has this common deficiency—that nature does not exist for it and that it lacks a living basis. On this account Spinoza's realism is as abstract as the idealism of Leibniz. Idealism is the soul of philosophy; realism is its body; only the two together constitute a living whole. Realism can never furnish the first principles but it must be the basis and the instrument by which idealism realizes itself and takes on flesh and blood. If a philosophy lacks this vital basis, usually a sign that the ideal principle was but weak from the outset, it then loses

itself in those systems whose attenuated concepts of *a-se-ity,* modality, etc., stand in the sharpest contrast to the vital power and fullness of reality. On the other hand, where the ideal principle really operates to a high degree but cannot discover a reconciling and mediating basis, it gives birth to a dreary and fanatic enthusiasm which breaks forth in self-mutilation or—as in the case of the priests of the Phrygian goddess— | in self-emasculation, which in philosophy is accomplished by the renunciation of reason and science. *357*

It seemed necessary to begin this treatise with the critique of essential concepts which have always, but especially in recent times, been confused. The foregoing remarks are therefore to be regarded as merely introductory to our actual investigation. We have already explained that a view such as would be fully adequate to the problem with which we are here concerned, could only be developed from the fundamental principles of a genuine philosophy of nature. We do not however deny that this correct view was long since present in individual minds.[a] But it was these very individuals who sought out the vital basis of nature, without fear of those terms of reproach—materialism, pantheism, etc.—which have ever been current against all genuine philosophy, and who were natural philosophers (in both senses of the word) in distinction to those dogmatists and abstract idealists who banished them as mystics.

The Philosophy of Nature of our time first established the distinction in science between Being insofar as it exists, and Being insofar as it is the mere basis of existence.[b] This distinction is as old as its first scientific presentation.[1] As this very point at which the Philosophy

[1] *Cf.* the *Journal for speculative Physics.* Vol. II, no. 2, § 54, Note, and also Note 1 to § 93, and the explanation on page 114.[c]

of Nature departs from the path of Spinoza most decisively has been disregarded, it could be maintained in Germany up to the present time that the metaphysical principles of this philosophy were identical with those of Spinoza. And although it is this distinction which at the same time brings about the most definite distinction between nature and God, this did not prevent the accusation that it constituted the confusion of God with nature. As the present investigation is based on the same distinction, the following may be remarked for its explication.

As there is nothing before or outside of God he must contain within himself the ground of his existence. All philosophies say this, but they | speak of this ground as a mere concept without making it something real and actual. This ground of his existence, which God contains [within himself], is not God viewed as absolute, that is insofar as he exists. For it is only the basis of his existence, it is *nature*—in God, inseparable from him, to be sure, but nevertheless distinguishable from him. By analogy, this relationship can be explicated through reference to the relation of gravitation and light in nature. Gravitation precedes light as its eternally dark basis which is itself not *actual* and flees into the night when light (which truly exists) appears. Even light does not completely break the seal by which gravity is held.[1] For this very reason gravity is neither the pure essence nor even the actual being of absolute identity, but it is only a consequence of its nature;[2] or else it is this identity when regarded in a specific degree. For that which appears as existing with respect to gravitation, itself belongs to the basis. And nature in general is therefore everything that lies beyond the absolute being of absolute identity.[3] With regard to

358

[1] *Ibid.* pp. 59, 60. [2] *Ibid.* p. 41. [3] *Ibid.* p. 114.

the precedence [of gravity over light], moreover, this is to be thought of neither as precedence in time nor as priority of essence. In the cycle whence all things come, it is no contradiction to say that that which gives birth to the one is, in its turn, produced by it. There is here no first and no last, since everything mutually implies everything else, nothing being the 'other' and yet no being being without the other. God contains himself in an inner basis of his existence, which, to this extent, precedes him as to his existence, but similarly God is prior to the basis as this basis, as such, could not be if God did not exist in actuality.

A consideration which proceeds from Things leads to the same distinction. First, the concept of immanence is completely to be set aside insofar as it is meant to express a dead conceptual inclusion of things in God. We recognize, rather, that the concept of | becoming is the only *359* one adequate to the nature of things. But the process of their becoming cannot be in God, viewed absolutely, since they are distinct from him *toto genere* or—more accurately in eternity. To be separate from God they would have to carry on this becoming on a basis different from him. But since there can be nothing outside God, this contradiction can only be solved by things having their basis in that within God which is not *God himself,*[1] i.e. in that which is the basis of his existence. If we wish to bring this Being nearer to us from a human standpoint, we may

[1] This is the only correct dualism, namely a dualism which at the same time admits a unity. Above was mentioned a modified dualism according to which the principle of evil does not stand alongside goodness but is subordinated to it. It is hardly to be feared that anyone will confuse the relationship here established with that dualism in which the subordinate is always an essentially evil principle and for this very reason remains incomprehensible with respect to its origin in God.

say: It is the longing which the eternal One feels to give birth to itself. This is not the One itself, but is co-eternal with it. This longing seeks to give birth to God, i.e. the unfathomable unity, but to this extent it has not yet the unity in its own self. Therefore, regarded in itself, it is also will: but a will within which there is no understanding, and thus not an independent and complete will, since understanding is actually the will in willing. Nevertheless it is a will of the understanding, namely the longing and desire thereof; not a conscious but a prescient will, whose prescience is understanding. We are speaking of the essence of longing regarded in and for itself, which we must view clearly although it was long ago submerged by the higher principle which had risen from it, and although we cannot grasp it perceptively but only spiritually, i.e. with our thoughts. Following the eternal act of self-revelation, the world as we now behold it, is all rule, order and form; but the unruly[a] lies ever in the depths as though it might again break through, and order and form nowhere appear to have been original, but it seems as though what had initially been unruly had been brought to order. This

360 is | the incomprehensible basis of reality in things, the irreducible remainder which cannot be resolved into reason[a] by the greatest exertion but always remains in the depths. Out of this which is unreasonable, reason[a] in the true sense is born. Without this preceeding gloom, creation would have no reality; darkness is its necessary heritage. Only God—the Existent himself—dwells in pure light; for he alone is self-born. Man's conceit opposes this origin from the depths and even seeks out moral reasons against it. Nevertheless we can think of nothing better fitted to drive man to strive towards the light with all energy, than

the consciousness of the deep night out of which he was raised into existence. The faint-hearted complaints that the unreasonable is in this way made into the root of reason, night into the beginning of light, are indeed partly based on a misunderstanding of the matter (since they do not grasp how the logical priority of reason and of essential being can be reconciled with the foregoing view), but these complaints express the actual system of contemporary philosophers who would like to make *fumum ex fulgere,* though even the most violent Fichtean precipitation is insufficient for this purpose. All birth is a birth out of darkness into light: the seed must be buried in the earth and die in darkness in order that the lovelier creature of light should rise and unfold itself in the rays of the sun. Man is formed in his mother's womb; and only out of the darkness of unreason (out of feeling, out of longing, the sublime mother of understanding) grow clear thoughts. We must imagine the primal longing in this way—turning towards reason, indeed, though not yet recognizing it, just as we longingly desire unknown, nameless excellence. This primal longing moves in anticipation like a surging, billowing sea, similar to the 'matter' of Plato, following some dark, uncertain law, incapable in itself of forming anything that can endure. But there is born in God himself an inward, imaginative response, corresponding to this longing, which is the first stirring of divine Being in its still dark depths. Through this response, God sees himself in his own image, since his imagination can have no other object than himself. | This image is the first in which God, viewed absolutely, is realized, though only in himself; it is in the beginning in God, and is the God-begotten God himself. This image is at one and the same *361* time, reason—the logic of that longing,[1] and the eternal Spirit which feels within it the Logos and the everlasting longing. This Spirit, moved by that Love which it itself is, utters the Word which then becomes creative and omnipotent Will combining reason and longing, and which informs nature, at first unruly, as its own element or instrument. The first effect of reason in nature is the separation of forces, which is the only way in which reason can unfold and develop the unity which had necessarily but unconsciously existed within nature, as in a seed. Just as in man there comes to light, when in the dark longing to create something, thoughts separate out of the chaotic confusion of thinking in which all are connected but each prevents the other from coming forth—so the unity appears which contains all within it and which had lain hidden in the depths. Or it is as in the case of the plant which escapes the dark fetters of gravity only as it unfolds and spreads its powers, developing its hidden unity as its substance becomes differentiated. For since this Being [of primal nature] is nothing else than the eternal basis of God's existence, it must contain within itself, though locked away, God's essence, as a light of life shining in the dark depths. But longing, roused by reason, now strives to preserve this light shining within it, and returns unto itself so that a basis of being might ever remain. In this way there is first formed something comprehensible and individuated; since reason, in the light which has appeared in the beginnings of nature, rouses longing (which is yearning to return into itself) to divide the forces (to surrender darkness) and in this very division brings out the unity enclosed in what was divided, the hidden light. And this [forming

[1] In the sense in which one finds a Logos in Logogriphs.[a]

of something comprehensible] does not occur by external discovery but through a genuine in-vention,[b] | since what arises in nature is conceived in it, or, still better, through revival, reason reviving the unity or idea concealed in the sundered depths. These forces which are divided but not completely separated in this division, are the material out of which the body will later be moulded; while the soul is that living nexus which arises, as the center of these forces in their division, from the depths of nature. Because primal reason elevates the soul as inner reality out of a basis which is independent of reason, the soul, on this account, remains independent of it, a separate and self-maintained being. 362

It can readily be seen that in the tension of longing necessary to bring things completely to birth the innermost nexus of the forces can only be released in a graded evolution, and at every stage in the division of forces there is developed out of nature a new being whose soul must be all the more perfect the more differentiatedly it contains what was left undifferentiated in the others. It is the task of a complete philosophy of nature to show how each successive process more closely approaches the essence of nature, until in the highest division of forces the innermost center is disclosed. For our present purpose only the following is essential. Every being which has arisen in nature in the manner indicated, contains a double principle which, however, is at bottom one and the same regarded from the two possible aspects. The first principle is the one by which they are separated from God or wherein they exist in the mere basis of things. But as an original unity exists between that which is in the basis, and what is prefigured in understanding, the second principle, which by its own nature is dark, is at the same time the very one which is revealed in light, and the two are one in every natural object, though only to a certain extent. For the process of creation consists only in an inner transmutation, or revelation in light of what was originally the principle of darkness since understanding or the light which occurs in nature is actually only searching in the depths for that light which is akin to it and is turned inward.[a] | The principle of darkness, insofar as it was drawn from the depths and is dark, is the self-will of creatures, but self-will, insofar as it has not yet risen to complete unity with light, as the principle of understanding cannot grasp it and is mere craving or desire, that is blind will. This self-will of creatures stands opposed to reason as universal will, and the latter makes use of the former and subordinates it to itself as a mere tool. But this will becomes one whole with the primal will or reason when, in the progressive transformation and division of all forces, there is totally revealed in light the inmost and deepest point of original darkness, in One Being. The will of this One Being, to the extent to which it is individual, is also a particular will, though in itself or as the center of all other particular wills it is one with the primal will or reason. This elevation of the most abysmal center into light, occurs in no creatures visible to us except in man. In man there exists the whole power of the principle of darkness and, in him too, the whole force of light. In him there are both centers—the deepest pit and the highest heaven. Man's will is the seed—concealed in eternal longing—of God, present as yet only in the depths,—the divine light of life locked in the deeps which God divined when he determined to will nature. Only in him (in man) did God love the world,—and it was this very image of God which was grasped in its center by longing when it opposed itself to light. By reason of the fact that man takes

363

his rise from the depths (that he is a creature) he contains a principle relatively independent of God. But just because this very principle is transfigured in light—without therefore ceasing to be basically dark—something higher, the *spirit,* arises in man. For the eternal spirit pronounces unity, or the Word, in nature. But the (real) Word, pronounced, exists only in the unity of light and darkness (vowel and consonant).[a] Now these two principles do indeed exist in all things, but without complete consonance because of the inadequacy of that which has been raised from the depths. Only in man, then, | is the Word completely articulate, which in all other creatures was held back and left unfinished. But in the articulate word the spirit reveals itself, that is God as existing, in act. Now inasmuch as the soul is the living identity of both principles, it is spirit; and spirit is in God. If, now, the identity of both principles were just as indissoluble in man as in God, then there would be no difference—that is, God as spirit would not be revealed. Therefore that unity which is indissoluble in God must be dissoluble in man—and this constitutes the possibility of good and evil.

364

We expressly say—"the possibility of evil," and for the present seek only to make comprehensible the divisibility of the principles. The reality of evil is the subject matter of quite another inquiry. That principle which rises up from the depths of nature and by which man is divided from God, is the selfhood in him; but by reason of its unity with the ideal principle, this becomes *spirit.* Selfhood, *as such,* is spirit; or man as an egocentric, particularized being (divorced from God) is spirit—the very relation [to God] constitutes personality.[a] But by reason of the fact that selfhood is spirit, it is at the same time raised from the level of the creature to a higher level.

It is will beholding itself in complete freedom, no longer the tool of the universal will operating in nature, but above and outside all nature. Spirit stands above light as in nature it raises itself above the unity of light and the principle of darkness. Thus, by being spirit, selfhood is free from both principles. However this selfhood, or self-will, only becomes spirit (and, accordingly, only becomes free and superior to nature) by being really transformed into the primal will (light), so that it indeed remains (as self-will) in the depths (because there must always be a basis)—just as in a transparent body the material which has been raised to identity with light does not therefore cease to be matter, the principle of darkness, except as being the bearer and, so to speak, the container of the higher principle of light. But selfhood can separate itself from light since it possesses spirit (because this is sovereign over light and darkness)—provided, indeed, it is not the spirit of eternal love itself. | Self-will may seek to be, as a particular will, that which it is only in its identity with the universal will. It may seek to be at the periphery that which it is only insofar as it remains at the center (just as the quiet will in the calm depths of nature is also universal will precisely because it stays in the depths). It may seek to be free as a creature, (for the will of creatures is, to be sure, beyond the depths, but in that case it is also a mere particular will, not free but restricted). Thus there takes place in man's will a division of his spiritualized selfhood from the light (as the spirit stands above light)—that is, a dissolution of the principles which in God are indissoluble. If, on the contrary, man's self-will remains in the depths as the central will, so that the divine relation of the principles persists (as, for example, the will in the center of nature never exalts itself above light but remains

365

below it as the basis in the depths), and if the spirit of love rules [in the will] in place of the spirit of dissension which wishes to divorce its own principle from the general principle, then the will exists in divine manner and condition. But that evil is this very exaltation of self-will is made clear from the following. Will, which deserts its supernatural status in order to make itself as general will also particular and creature will, at one and the same time, strives to reverse the relation of the principles, to exalt the basis above the cause, and to use that spirit which it received only for the center, outside the center and against the creature, which leads to disorganization within itself and outside itself. Man's will may be regarded as a nexus of living forces; as long as it abides in its unity with the universal will these forces remain in their divine measure and balance. But hardly does self-will move from the center which is its station, than the nexus of forces is also dissolved; in its place a merely particular will rules which can no longer unite the forces among themselves as before, but must therefore strive to form or compose a special and peculiar life out of the now separate forces, an in surgent host of desires and passions | — since every individual force is also an obsession and passion. This is possible inasmuch as the first nexus of forces, the foundation of nature, persists even in evil. As a genuine life could only exist in the original relationship, there thus arises a life which is indeed a life, but is false, a life of lies, a growth of disquiet and corruption. The most appropriate comparison is here offered by disease,[a] which is the true counterpart of evil and sin, as it constitutes that disorder which entered nature through a misuse of freedom. Disease of the whole organism can never exist without the hidden forces of the depths being unloosed; it occurs when

366

the irritable principle which ought to rule as the innermost tie of forces in the quiet deep, activates itself, or when Archaos is provoked to desert his quiet residence at the center of things and steps forth into the surroundings. So, on the other hand, all radical cure consists in the reestablishment of the relation of the periphery to the center, and the transition from disease to health can really only take place through its opposite, that is through the restoration of separate and individual life to the inner light of the being, whence there recurs the division (crisis). Local disease also occurs only because some entity whose freedom or life exists only so that it may remain in the whole, strives to exist for itself. Disease is indeed nothing essential and is actually only an illusion of life and the mere meteoric appearance of it—a swaying between being and non-being—but nonetheless announces itself in feeling as something very real. Just so is the case of evil.

In recent times this only correct conception of evil as consisting of a positive perversion or reversal of the principles, has been advanced especially by Franz Baader[b] who has expounded it through profound physical analogies, especially those of disease.[1] | All other explanations of

367

[1] In the treatise *On the Assertion that there can be no bad Use of Reason,* in the *Morgenblatt,* 1807, No. 197; and, *Concerning* | *Solids and Liquids,* in the *Annuals of Medicine as Science,* Vol. III, No. 2. For purposes of comparison and further explication we quote here the relevant Note at the conclusion of this treatise, page 203: "An instructive clue is here given by common fire (as wild, consuming, burning flame) in distinction to the so-called organic beneficial warmth of life, since *in the latter* fire and water come together in a single (growing) basis or enter into conjunction, whereas *in the former* case they separate in dissension. Now neither fire nor water existed as such, that is as separate spheres in the organic process, but the former existed as center (*mysterium*) and the latter existed openly or as its periphery; and it was just the unlocking, elevation and influencing of the former

367n

evil leave the understanding and moral consciousness alike dissatisfied. They all rest at bottom on the denial of evil as a positive antithesis, and its reduction to the so-called *malum metaphysicum* or the negative concept of the imperfection of the creature. It was impossible, says Leibniz, that God should grant man all perfection without making him himself God; the same applies to created beings in general; and on this account it was necessary to bring about various grades of perfection and all sorts of limitation thereof. If one asks what is the source of evil, the answer is: in the ideal nature of the creature, insofar as it is dependent on the eternal verities contained in divine reason but not on God's will. The realm of eternal verities is the ideal cause of evil and good, and must be put in the place of the | 'matter' of the ancients.[1] There are, to be sure, he says in another place, two principles, but both exist in God and they are reason and will. Reason yields the principle of evil, though it does not thereby itself become evil; for it presents all natures as they are in accordance with the eternal verities; it contains in itself the basis for the admission of evil, whereas will is directed only towards the

368

which, together with the restriction of the latter, brought about disease and death. Thus the ego, or individuality, is indeed in general the basis, foundation or natural center of every creature's life; but as soon as it ceases to be the ministering center and enters as sovereign into the periphery, it burns in it like Tantalus's malice in its selfishness and egoism. ⊙ now turns into ○—that is: that dark center of nature is locked away in a single place in the planetary system, lies latent there, and for this very reason serves as the bearer of light for the entrance of the higher system (the entering ray of light, or the revelation of the ideal). Just on this account this place is then the open point (sun—heart—eye) in the system—and if the dark center of nature rose up or opened itself here too, the point of light would, *eo ipso,* disappear; light would turn into darkness in the system, or the sun would be extinguished."

[1] *Tentam. theod.* Opp. T.I., p. 136[a]

good.[2] This sole possibility was not of God's making, since reason is not its own cause.[3] This distinction of reason and will as two principles in God, by means of which the original possibility of evil is made independent of divine will, is in accord with the suggestive thought of this man, [Leibniz]; and the conception of reason (divine wisdom) as something to which God himself is related passively rather than actively, points to something deeper. Nevertheless the evil which could be derived from this exclusively ideal basis turns out to be something merely passive—limitation, insufficiency, deprivation—concepts which are completely at odds with the actual nature of evil. For the mere consideration of the fact that man, the most perfect of all visible creatures, is alone capable of evil, shows that this basis can by no means consist of insufficiency or deprivation. According to the Christian view, the devil was not the most limited but rather the least limited of creatures.[4] Imperfection in the general | metaphysical sense, is not the common character of evil, as it often manifests itself united with an excellence of individual powers which much less frequently accompanies the good. The basis of evil must therefore not only

369

[2] *Ibid.* p. 240

[3] *Ibid.* p. 387

[4] In this connection it is striking that the scholastics were not the first to designate evil as a mere privation, but that a number of the earlier Church Fathers, especially Augustine, did so. Particularly noteworthy is the passage *Contr. Jul.* L. 1, C. III: Quaerunt ex nobis, unde sit malum? Respondemus ex bono, sed non summo, ex bonis igitur orta sunt mala. Mala enim omnia participant ex bono, merum enim et ex omni parte tale dari repugnat.—Haud vero difficulter omnia expediet, qui conceptum mali semel recte formaverit, *eumque semper defectum aliquem involvere attenderit,* perfectionem autem omnimodam incommunicabiliter possidere Deum; neque magis possibile | esse, creaturam illimitatam adeoque independentem creari, quam creari alium Deum.

369n

be founded on something inherently positive, but rather on the highest positive being which nature contains. This, indeed, is the case in accordance with our views since it lies in the manifested center or primal will of the first basis. Leibniz tries in every way to make comprehensible how evil could arise from a natural insufficiency. The will, he says, strives towards the good in general, and must seek perfection whose highest measure is in God; but if it remains entangled in the voluptuousness of the senses with a loss of higher value, this very lack of further effort is the privation which constitutes evil. Otherwise, he suggests, evil requires a special principle as little as do cold or darkness. That which is affirmative in evil is only incidental, like force and efficacy in cold; freezing water cracks the strongest container, and cold nonetheless actually consists in a decrease of motion.[1] However since deprivation is nothing in itself and, in order even to become noticeable, requires something positive in which it becomes apparent, the difficulty now occurs of explaining the positive factor which must after all be assumed in evil. As Leibniz can only derive this from God, he finds himself obliged to make God the cause of that which is material in sin, and to ascribe only its formal aspect to the original limitation of the creature. He seeks to explicate this relationship by means of the conception which Kepler discovered, of the natural inertia of matter. This, he says, is the complete picture of an original limitation of the creature, which precedes all activity. If two different bodies of unequal mass are moved by the same impulse with unequal velocities, | then the cause of the slowness of the motion of the one is not in the impulse but in the peculiar tendency 370

[1] *Tentam. theod.* p. 242[a]

to inertia innate in the matter, that is, in the inner limitation or imperfection of matter.[1] But in this connection it should be remarked that inertia itself cannot be thought of as a mere deprivation, but that it is indeed something positive, namely an expression of the inner selfhood of the body, the force through which it seeks to maintain itself in its independence. We do not deny that metaphysical finitude can be made comprehensible in this way, but we do deny that finitude in itself is evil.[2]

This type of explanation is after all drawn from that lifeless conception of the positive, in accordance with which only deprivation can be contrasted with it. There is, however, an intermediate concept which provides a real contrast to it and which is far removed from the concept of mere negation. This is derived from the relationship of the whole to the individual, of unity to multiplicity, or however one wishes to express it. The positive is always the whole or unity; that which is contrasted with it is division of the whole, discord, ataxia of forces. The identical elements which existed in the unified whole are in the divided whole; the matter in both is the same—from this aspect evil is no more limited or worse than good; but the formal aspect of the two is totally different and it is this very form which comes from the essence or positive factor itself. Thus there must necessarily be a positive character in evil as in the good, but in the former it is one opposed to the good, which transforms its normal temperature into distemper.[b] It is impossible for dogmatic philosophy to recognize this character since it has no

[1] *Ibid.* P. I. § 30[a]

[2] For the same reason every other explanation of finitude, for instance by the concept of relations, must be inadequate as an explanation of evil. Evil is not derived from finitude in itself, but from finitude which has been exalted to independent being.

conception of personality, that is of selfhood elevated to spirituality, but | only an abstract concept of the infinite and the finite. Thus if someone wished to reply that discord is precisely a privation, namely a deprivation of unity, nevertheless this concept would be insufficient even if the general conception of deprivation contained the concept of the dissolution or division of unity. For the division of forces is not in itself discord but the false unity of forces which can only be called a division in relation to true unity. If unity is completely dissolved, then conflict is thereby dissolved too. The end of disease is death, and no single tone makes a discord by itself. But just to explain this false unity requires something positive which must accordingly and of necessity be assumed in evil, but which will remain inexplicable as long as a root of freedom is not recognized in the independent basis of nature. *371*

The Platonic view, insofar as we can judge it, will best be discussed in considering the question of the actuality of evil. The notions of our age, which takes a far easier view of this point and carries its humanitarianism to the extent of denying evil, have not even the slightest connection with such ideas.[a] According to current views the sole basis of evil lies in the world of the senses or in animality or the earthly principle, since they do not contrast Heaven with Hell, as would be proper, but with Earth. This notion is the natural outcome of the doctrine in accordance with which freedom consists in the mere mastery of the intelligent principle over the desires and inclinations of the senses, and the good is derived from pure reason. Accordingly it is obvious that evil can have no freedom (since the inclinations of the senses are here sovereign) or—to speak more correctly—evil is completely lost sight of. For the feebleness and inefficacy of the

reasonable principle can indeed be a basis for the lack of good and virtuous actions, but it cannot be a basis for actions that are positively bad and opposed to virtue. But if it is granted that passion or a passive attitude to ex-
372 ternal impressions | involves evil actions with a kind of necessity, then, in performing them, man himself would be only passive. That is, evil would have no meaning from the point of view of the agent (i.e. subjectively) and as whatever follows from natural determination, objectively considered too, cannot be evil, evil would have no meaning at all. But to say that the reasonable principle is ineffective in evil, explains nothing either. For why does it not exert its power? If it prefers to be ineffective, then the basis of evil is in this preference and not in the world of the senses. Or if it can in no way conquer the opposing power of the latter, then we have here mere feebleness and insufficiency but nowhere evil. Thus, in accordance with this explanation there is but one will (if, indeed, it can be so called) and no dual will. And the adherents of this view could in this regard be called Monotheletes, for since the names of Arian, etc., have happily been introduced into philosophic criticism we can also take this name from Church History, though in a different sense. But just as it is nowise the intelligent principle, or the principle of light, in itself which operates in the good, but only this principle combined with selfhood, that is, elevated to spirit; in the same way evil is not derived from the principle of finitude in itself, but only from the dark or selfish principle which has been brought into intimacy with the center. And just as there is an ardor for the good, there is also an enthusiasm for evil. That dark principle is indeed effective in animals too, as in every other natural being; but in them it has not yet been born to light as in

man, it is not *spirit* and understanding but blind passion and desire; in short no degeneration, no division of principles is possible here where there is as yet no absolute or personal unity. In animal instinct the unconscious and the conscious are united only in a specific and definite fashion which for this very reason is unalterable. For because of this, because they are only relative expressions of unity, they are subject to it, and the force which operates in the depths receives the unity of the principles which is appropriate to it in ever the same measure. Animals can never | escape from unity, whereas man can deliberately cut the eternal nexus of forces. Wherefore Franz Baader is right in saying that it would be desirable if the rottenness in man could only go as far as animality; but unfortunately man can only stand above or beneath animals.[a][1]

373

We have sought to deduce the concept and the possibility of evil from first principles, and to discover the general basis of this doctrine which lies in the distinction between existence and that which is the ground of existence.[2] But possibility does not include actuality, and the latter is really the chief subject in question. And indeed what has to be explained is not simply how evil comes to be real in individual men, but its universal effectiveness and how it could have burst forth from creation as an unmistakable

[1] In the above mentioned treatise in the *Morgenblatt,* 1807, p. 786.

[2] Augustine says, in opposition to emanation: Naught can come forth out of God's substance except God; therefore the creature was made out of Nothing, whence its corruptibility and insufficiency result. (*De lib. arb.* L. I, C. 2). That "Nothing" has now long since been the cross of reason. A clue is provided by the scriptural expression: Man is ἐκ τῶν μὴ ὄντων—man is made out of that which is not, just like the famous μὴ ὄν of the ancients, which like the Creation out of Nothing might first receive a positive meaning through the above distinction.

general principle, everywhere battling against the good. Since it is undeniably real at least as a general contrast, there can indeed be no doubt from the outset that it was necessary for God's revelation. This, indeed, can also be deduced from what has been said before. For if God, as spirit, is the indivisible unity of the two principles, and this same unity is actual only in man's spirit, then if it were just as indissoluble in him as in God, man could not be distinguished from God at all; he would disappear in God and there would be no revelation and no stirring of love. For every nature can be revealed only in its opposite —love in hatred, unity in strife. If there were no division of the principles, then unity could not | manifest its omnipotence; if there were no conflict then love could not become real. Man has been placed on that summit where he contains within him the source of self-impulsion towards good and evil in equal measure; the nexus of the principles within him is not a bond of necessity but of freedom. He stands at the dividing line; whatever he chooses will be his act, but he cannot remain in indecision because God must necessarily reveal himself and because nothing at all in creation can remain ambiguous. Nonetheless it seems as though he could not escape his indecision, just because it is indecision. There must therefore be a general cause of temptation, a solicitation to evil, even if it were only to bring the principles within him to life, that is, to make him conscious of them. Now it seems as though the solicitation to evil could itself only come from an evil first cause. And the assumption of such a basis seems unavoidable anyway, a quite correct exegesis of Platonic "matter," which was an entity originally struggling against God and therefore inherently evil. As long as this part of the Pla-

374

tonic doctrine remains, as up to now, in darkness,[1] a definite judgment regarding this matter is indeed impossible. The foregoing considerations, however, make clear in what sense it can be said of the irrational principle that it is in opposition to reason or to unity and order, without on this account regarding it as an *evil* first cause. We can presumably explain in this way too, the Platonic dictum that evil is derived *from primal nature.* For all evil strives back towards chaos, that is, towards that condition in which the initial center had not yet been subordinated to light, and is an effervescence of the center of still irrational longing. Be that as it may, we have proved once and for all that evil, as such, can only arise in created beings, since here alone light and darkness, or the | two principles, can be united in a way capable of division. The first cause of all can never be evil in itself, as there is no duality of the principles in it. But neither can we presuppose a created spirit, itself fallen, which solicited man to fall: for the very question, at this point, is how evil arose in a created being. Therefore nothing is given us for the explanation of evil except the two principles in God. God as spirit (the eternal nexus of the two) is purest love, but in love there can never be a will to evil, and just as little can there be in the ideal principle. But God himself requires a foundation in order that he may be; only this is not outside him but within him; and he has in him a *nature* which though it belongs to him himself, is, nonetheless, different from him. The will of love

375

[1] We wish that it might sometime be cleared up by the able exponent of Plato[a] or still sooner by the doughty Böckh[b], who has given us the best reason to hope for it through his remarks in connection with his exposition of Platonic "harmony" and through the announcement of his edition of the *Timaeus.*

and the will of the basis are two different wills, each existing by itself; but the will of love cannot withstand the will of the basis, nor can it elevate the latter, since in that case it would have to strive against itself. For the basis must function so that love may be, and must operate independently of love so that the latter may exist in reality. Thus if love wished to break the will in the depths, it would be in conflict with itself, it would be in disunion with itself and would no longer be love. This allowing of the basis to function is the only thinkable conception of permissibility, whereas permissibility is entirely inappropriate in its usual application to man. Neither, to be sure, can the will of the basis destroy love, nor does it desire this, though it often seems so; for it must be a will of its own and peculiar bent, turned away from love, so that love may appear in its omnipotence when, despite all, it breaks through the will of the basis, like light through darkness. The basis is only a will to revelation, but just in order that the latter may come to pass the former must call forth distinctiveness and contrast. The will of love and the will of the basis thus become one, just through the fact that they are divided and that from the very beginning each functions for itself. Therefore the will of the basis excites the self-will of the creature from the first creation, so that when the spirit then arises as the will of | love it may find an opponent in which it can realize itself. *376*

The aspect of all nature convinces us that this excitation occurred, by means of which alone all life achieved differentiation and distinctiveness to the last degree. The irrational and accidental element which reveals itself as connected with what is necessary in the formation of all beings, especially organic ones, proves that it was not merely a geometric necessity which operated here, but that freedom, spirit and self-will played their part too. To be sure, wherever passion and desire are, there is already a kind of freedom. And no one will believe that the desire which constitutes the basis of every particular life in nature, and the instinct of self-preservation (preservation not in general but of this specific entity) were super-added to the already finished creature—but rather that they were themselves the creative factor. The empirical concept of the basis, too, which will assume an important role in all natural science, must, if scientifically thought out, also lead to a conception of selfhood and individuality. But in nature they are accidental determinations which are explicable only by an excitation of the irrational or dark principle of creatures in primal creation, explicable only in terms of activated selfhood. Whence are there in nature unmistakable premonitions of evil alongside pre-established moral relationships, if the power of evil was only aroused by man? Whence the phenomena which excite a general, natural repugnance even without regard to their being dangerous to man?[1] It is by no means apparent as an original necessity that all organic beings | should approach dissolution; the nexus of forces which compose life could *377*

[1] Thus the close connection which the imagination of all peoples, (especially all fables and religions of the Orient) makes between the serpent and evil, is certainly not unfounded. Indeed the complete development of the accessory organs, which has advanced to its highest stage in man, already indicates the independence of the will from the passions, or a relationship of the center to the periphery, which alone is really healthy. In this relation the center has withdrawn in its freedom and circumspection and has separated itself from what is merely instrumental (peripheral). On the other hand when the accessory organs have not developed | or are altogether lacking, then the center has entered the periphery, or it is the circle without a dot in the center, in the passage cited above (in the note) from Franz Baader. *377n*

just as well, by its own nature, be indissoluble; and, if anything, a creature which restores what has become imperfect in it by means of its own forces, seems destined to be a *perpetuum mobile.* However, in nature, evil declares itself only by its effects; only at nature's goal can it itself break forth in its immediate appearance. For as in the beginning of creation, which was nothing other than the birth of light, the dark principle had to be there as its basis so that light could be raised out of it (as the actual out of the merely potential); so there must be another basis for the birth of spirit, and hence a second principle of darkness, which must be as much higher than the former as the spirit is higher than light. This principle is precisely the spirit of evil which has been awakened in creation through the arousing of the dark natural basis, —that is the *disunion* of light and darkness— to which the spirit of love is now opposed as a higher ideal, as before light was opposed to the unruly movement of nature in its beginnings. For as selfhood has made light, or the Word, its own in evil, and for this very reason appears as a higher basis of darkness, so the Word which has been sent into the world in opposition to evil, must take on humanity or selfhood and itself become personal. This occurs only through revelation (in the most definite sense of the word) which must have identically the same stages as the first manifestation in nature—in such a way namely, that here, too, the highest summit of revelation is man, but the exemplary and divine Man, he who in the beginning was with God, and in whom all other things and man himself were created. The birth of spirit is the realm of history, as the birth of light is the realm of nature. The same stages of creation | which exist in the latter are also in the former; and the one is the symbol

378

and explanation of the other. The identical principle which was the basis of the first creation is here again the germ and seed, only in a higher form, from which a higher world is developed. For evil is, of course, nothing other than the primal basis of existence insofar as it strives towards actualization in created beings, and thus it is in fact only the higher potency of the basis operating in nature. But just as this is eternally only the basis, without itself being, so evil can never attain realization and only serves as basis, in order that the good may develop from it, by its own power, and may through its basis be independent of and separate from God; wherein God may have and behold himself, and which may exist as such (as independent), [yet] in God. But just as the undivided power of the primal basis is only recognized in man as the inner basis or center of an individual, so, too, in history, evil at first remains concealed in the depths, and the age of guilt or sin is preceded by an age of innocence or unconsciousness of sin. The primal basis of nature may have operated alone long before, and, through the divine forces contained within it, it may itself have attempted a creation which, however, since the bond of love was lacking, always relapsed in the end back into chaos (as is perhaps indicated by the series of species which were destroyed before the present creation and did not return) until the word of love went forth and with it enduring creation took its start. In just the same way the spirit of love did not reveal itself at once in history, but God rather allowed the basis to operate independently, because he felt the will of the basis to be the will towards his revelation and recognized, in accordance with his providence, that a basis independent of him (as spirit) would have to be the basis of his existence. Or, to express it differently, God himself moved

only in accordance with his nature and not in accordance with his heart or in accordance with love. Now because the basis also contained within itself the whole of the divine Being, only not as unity, there could only be in-
379 dividual divine | beings which reigned in this self-operation of the basis. This primeval time thus commences with the golden age, of which only a feeble memory has remained in legend for the present race of man, a period of blessed indifference in which there was neither good nor evil.[a] There then followed the age of sovereign gods and heroes, or the omnipotence of nature, in which the basis showed what it was capable of in itself. At that time understanding and wisdom came to men only from the depths, the power of oracles issuing from the earth guided and formed their lives; all the divine forces of the deep ruled upon Earth and, as mighty princes, occupied secure thrones. The age of the greatest glorification of nature dawned in the visible beauty of the gods and in the glamor of art and significant science, until the principle operating in the deep at last stepped forth as world-conquering, seeking to subordinate all to itself and to establish a firm and enduring world dominion. But because the principle of the depths can never give birth for itself to true and complete unity, the time comes in which all this glory dissolves and the beautiful body of the foregoing world decays as through horrible disease, and finally chaos again ensues. Even earlier and before the total destruction has arrived, the powers which reigned in that whole take on the nature of evil spirits, just as the same forces which were beneficent guardian spirits of life in the time of health, become malignant and poisonous natures when dissolution approaches.[b] The belief in gods disappears and a false magic combined with incantations and theurgic formulae seeks

to call back the fleeing spirits and to appease the evil ones. Feeling, in advance, the coming of light, the gathering of the deep grows constantly more apparent, and at once draws all forces from indetermination to meet light in full opposition. As the thunderstorm is brought on by the mediation of the sun, but immediately through an opposing force of the Earth, so the spirit of evil (whose meteoric nature we have already explained) is aroused through the approach of the good, not by means of a participation but rather through a partition of forces.[c] Thus it is only with the decisive | coming of the good that evil too becomes manifest decisively and as such (not as though it only now arose, but because the contrast is only now given in which it can appear in its totality and as itself). And again, it is just the moment at which the Earth for a second time becomes barren and void which becomes the moment for the birth of the higher light of the spirit which existed from the very beginning of the world but was not encompassed by the darkness that moved unto itself, and was still hidden in incomplete revelation. Indeed, in order to encounter personal and spiritual evil, light appears in personal and human form, and comes as mediator in order to reestablish the relationship between creation and God on the highest level. For only personality can make whole what is personal, and God must become Man in order that man may be brought back to God. Only by restoring the relation of the basis to God is the possibility of wholeness (salvation) regained. Its beginning is a condition of luminous insight which comes about through divine designation of individual men (as organs chosen for this purpose)—a time of signs and portents in which divine powers counteract the demonic, everywhere manifest, and unity assuages the division of forces. At last there results

380

the crisis in the *turba gentium* which overflow the foundations of the ancient world as once the waters of the beginning again covered the creations of primeval time, in order to make possible a second creation—a new division of the peoples and of tongues, a new realm in which the living Word enters as a firm and enduring center in battle against chaos, and a declared state of war between good and evil commences, which continues to the end of the present time and in which God reveals himself as spirit, that is as real actuality.[1]

There is, therefore, a *universal* evil, even if it is not active from the beginning but is only aroused in God's revelation through the reaction | of the basis, and indeed never reaches realization, but is nonetheless constantly striving towards it. Only after recognizing evil in its universal character is it possible to comprehend good and evil in man too. For if evil was already aroused in the first creation and was finally developed into a general principle through the self-centered operation of the basis,[a] then man's natural inclination to evil seems at once explicable, because the disorder of forces once having entered creatures through the awakening of self-will is already communicated to man at birth. Indeed the dark ground operates incessantly in individual man too, and rouses egotism and a particularized will just in order that the will of love may arise in contrast to it. It is God's will to universalize everything, to lift it to unity with light or to preserve it therein; but the will of the deep is to particularize everything or to make it creature-like. It wishes differentiation[b] only so that identity may become evident to itself and to the will of the

381

[1] Compare with this entire section the author's *Lectures on the Method of Academic Study, VIII. Lecture on the Historic Construction of Christendom.*

deep. Therefore it necessarily reacts against freedom as against what is above the creature, and awakens in it the desire for what is creature—just as he who is seized by dizziness on a high and precipitous summit seems to hear a mysterious voice calling to him to plunge down, or as in the ancient tale, the irresistible song of the sirens sounded out of the deep to draw the passing mariner down into the whirlpool. Intrinsically the combination in man of the universal will with a particular will seems to be a contradiction; their union seems difficult if not impossible. The terror of life drives man out of the center in which he was created; for being the lucid and pure essence of all will this is consuming fire for each particular will; in order to be able to live in it man must mortify all egotism, which almost makes necessary the attempt to leave it and to enter the periphery in order to seek peace for his selfhood there. Thence comes the general necessity of sin and death as the real mortification of egotism, through which all human will must pass as through a fire in order to be purified. Notwithstanding this general | necessity, evil ever remains man's own choice; the basis cannot cause evil as such, and every creature falls through its own guilt. But just how the decision for good or evil comes to pass in the individual man, that is still wrapped in total darkness and seems to require a special investigation. *382*

Up to the present we have, in any case, attended less closely to the formal side of freedom, although an insight into it seems to be connected with no less difficulty than the explanation of the concept of its reality.

For the usual conception of freedom, according to which it consists of a completely undetermined power to will either one of two contradictory opposites without determining reasons, simply because it is desired,—this usual conception has indeed in its favor the original indecision of essential human nature, but when applied to individual actions it leads to the greatest inconsistencies. To be able to decide for A or —A without any motivating reasons would, to tell the truth, only be a privilege to act entirely unreasonably, and would not indeed distinguish man in any worthy way from the well known beast of Buridan which, in the opinion of the advocates of this conception of free will, had to starve between two equally distant, equally large and altogether similar stacks of hay just because it did not have the privilege of arbitrary choice. The only proof of this conception consists in an appeal to the fact that, for instance, it is in everyone's power to draw back or extend his arm without further reason. For if one declares that he extends it just to prove his freedom to choose, he could, after all, do this just as well by drawing it back; his interest in proving the proposition could only determine him to do one of the two; thus an equilibrium is here manifest, etc. This is a thoroughly bad method of proof because it deduces the non-existence of a determining cause from ignorance about it. But this argument could here be applied in just the opposite way—for precisely | 383 where ignorance enters, determination all the more certainly takes place. The chief thing is that this conception makes individual actions completely accidental, and in this respect it has very rightly been compared to the accidental swerving of the atoms which Epicurus invented for the same purpose in physics, namely in order to escape Fate. But accident is impossible and contradicts reason as well as the necessary unity of the whole; and if freedom cannot be saved except by making actions totally accidental, then it cannot be saved at all. To this system of the equilibrium of choice, determinism (or, according to Kant, predeterminism) is opposed, indeed quite justly, in asserting the empirical necessity of all actions on the ground that each of them was determined by motives or other causes which lay in the past and which are no longer in our control at the time of the action. Both systems adopt essentially the same standpoint, except that if there were no higher position the second would undeniably deserve preference. Both are alike ignorant of that higher necessity which is equally far removed from accident and from compulsion or external determination but which is, rather, an inner necessity which springs from the essence of the active agent itself. Incidentally, nothing in the least is gained by all the improvements which have been appended to determinism, such as Leibniz's amendment that motivating causes might dispose but not determine the will.

It was, indeed, Idealism which first raised the doctrine of freedom into that realm in which it alone can be understood. In consequence of it the intelligible essence of everything, and particularly of man, is outside of all causal connections as it is outside or beyond all time. Therefore it can never be determined by anything which preceded, since it itself rather takes precedence over all else which is or develops within it, not in time but in terms of its concept as an absolute unity whose totality and completeness must ever be actual in order that a specific act or determination may be possible in it. For we | are expressing the *384* Kantian conception not exactly in his words but in just such a way as, we believe, it must be expressed in order to be understood. But if this conception is accepted then the following too seems to have been correctly inferred. Free activity follows immediately from the intelligible nature of man. But it is necessarily an activity of determinate character; for instance—to refer to what is nearest at hand—it must be a good or bad activity. However there is no transition from the absolutely undetermined to the determined. The notion that an intelligible being could determine itself from sheer and utter indetermination without any reason, leads back to the above mentioned system of the equilibrium of choice. In order to be able to determine itself it would have to be already determined in itself; not indeed from the outside, since this would be in contradiction to its nature, nor from within by any merely accidental or empirical necessity, since all this (psychological as well as physical) is subordinate to it. But it would have to be determined by its own essence, that is by its own nature. This essence is no indefinite generality but definitely the intelligible essence of this specific human being. The saying, *determinatio est negatio,* does not in any way apply to this sort of determination, since this is itself one with the reality and concept of this essence, thus really being the essential element in the essence. The intelligible being, therefore, insofar as it acts absolutely and with full freedom, can as certainly only act according to its own inner nature. Or the activity can follow from its inner nature only in accordance with the law of identity, and with absolute necessity which is also the only absolute freedom. For only that is free which acts according to the laws of its own inner being and is not determined by anything else either within it or outside it.

This view of the matter yields at least one advantage in that it removes the inconsistent notion of the contingency of individual acts. This must be established in every higher view as well: that an individual act is the consequence of an inner necessity of the free being and accordingly is itself necessary. But this necessity must not be confused, as still happens, with an empirical necessity based on compulsion (which is | itself only a veiled contingency). But what is this inner necessity of the Being itself? This is the point at which necessity and freedom must be united if they can be united at all. If this Being were a dead being and, for man, a mere datum, then since its activity would only ensue from necessity, imputability and all freedom would be vitiated. But just this inner necessity is itself freedom; man's being is essentially *his own deed.* Necessity and freedom interpenetrate as one being which appears as the one or the other only as regarded from various aspects; in itself it is freedom, but formally regarded, necessity. The Ego, said Fichte, is its own deed; consciousness posits itself—but the Ego is nothing other than this, nothing but the positing itself. However this consciousness, insofar as it is thought of as mere self-apprehension or knowledge of the Ego, is not even the primary position, and like all mere knowledge it presupposes the actual 'Being.' But this Being which is assumed as prior to knowledge is no being, even if it is not knowledge either; it is real self-positing, it is a primal and basic willing which makes itself into something and is the basis and foundation of all essence. 385

But in a way far more definite than this general sense, these truths have an immediate relation to man. In original creation, as has been shown, man is an undetermined entity (which may be mythologically presented as a condition antecedent to this life, a state of innocence and of initial bliss). He alone can determine himself. But this determination cannot occur in time; it occurs outside of time altogether and hence it coincides with the first creation even though as an act differentiated from it. Man, even though born in time, is nonetheless a creature of creation's beginning (the centrum). The act which determines man's life in time does not itself belong in time but in eternity.

Moreover it does not precede life in time but occurs throughout time (untouched | by it) as an act eternal by its own nature. Through it man's life extends to the beginning of creation, since by means of it he is also more than creature, free and himself eternal beginning. Though this idea may seem beyond the grasp of common ways of thought, there is in every man a feeling which is in accord with it, as if each man felt that he had been what he is from all eternity, and had in no sense only come to be so in time. Thus, the undeniable necessity of all actions notwithstanding, and though everyone must admit, if he observes himself, that he is in no wise good or bad by accident or choice, yet a bad person, for instance, seems to himself anything but compelled (since compulsion can only be felt in becoming, not in being) but performs his acts wilfully, not against his will. That Judas became a traitor to Christ, neither he nor any creature could alter; nonetheless he betrayed Christ not under compulsion but willingly and with full freedom.[1] The same thing is true of a good man—namely that he is not good by accident or choice, but nonetheless is so little under compulsion that no coercion, indeed not even the very gates of hell, would be capable of overpowering his disposition. To be sure, this free act which becomes necessity cannot occur in consciousness, insofar as it is mere self-awareness and only ideal consciousness, since the act precedes it as it precedes being and indeed produces it. But, nevertheless, it is not at all an act of which no consciousness remains to man. Thus someone, who perhaps to excuse a wrong act, says: "Well, that's the way I am"—is himself well aware that he is so

386

[1] Luther correctly writes to this effect in the tract, *De servo arbitrio,* even if he did not comprehend in the right way the union of such unavoidable necessity with freedom of action.

because of his own fault, however correct he may be in thinking that it would have been impossible for him to act differently. How often does it not happen that a man shows a tendency to evil from childhood on, from a time when, empirically viewed, we can scarcely attribute freedom and deliberation to him, so that we can anticipate | 387 that neither punishment nor teaching will move him, and who subsequently really turns out to be the twisted limb which we anticipated in the bent twig. But no one questions his responsibility, and all are as convinced of the guilt of this person as one could be if every single act had been in his control. This common judgment of a tendency to do evil, (a tendency which in its origin is entirely unconscious and even irresistible) as being a free deed, points to an act and thus to a life before this life. Only it must not just be thought of as prior in time, since what is intelligible is altogether outside time. In creation there is the greatest harmony, and nothing is so separate and sequent as we must represent it, but the subsequent cooperates in what precedes it and everything occurs at the same time in one magic stroke. Therefore man, who here appears as fixed and determined, took on a specific form in first creation and is born as that which he is from eternity, since this primal act determined even the nature and condition of his corporealization. The greatest obstacle to the doctrine of freedom has ever been the relation of the assumed accidental nature of human conduct to the unity of the world-whole as previously planned in divine reason. Thus there came the assumption of predestination, since neither God's prescience nor actual providence could be relinquished. The authors of the doctrine of predestination felt that human conduct must have been determined from eternity. However they did not seek this determination in the eternal act contemporaneous with creation, which constitutes the being of man itself, but in an absolute (i.e. wholly unfounded) decision of God through which one individual was predetermined to damnation, the other to blessedness; and thus they destroyed the root of freedom. We, too, declare a predestination, but in an entirely different sense, namely thus: as man acts here so he has acted since eternity and already in the beginning of creation. His conduct does not *come to be*, as he himself, | as a moral being, does not *come to be*; but it is eternal in its nature. In this, that oft heard distressing question also disappears: why is just this man determined to act wickedly and viciously while another acts, by contrast, piously and righteously? For this question assumes that man was from the very beginning not act and deed, and that as a spiritual being he has an existence prior to and independent of his will,—which, as has been shown, is impossible.

388

When, through the reaction of the depths to revelation, evil in general had once been aroused in creation, man from eternity took his stand in egotism and selfishness; and all who are born are born with the dark principle of evil attached to them, even though this evil is raised to self-consciousness only through the entrance of its opposite. As man now is, the good, the light as it were, can be produced only out of this dark principle through divine transmutation. Only he could gainsay this original evil in man who has but superficially come to know man in himself and in others. This evil, though it is entirely independent of freedom with respect to present empirical life, was at its source man's own deed, and hence the only original sin. The same cannot be said of that equally undeniable disorder of forces which spread as a contagion after the initial corruption. For it is not the passions which are in themselves evil, nor are we battling merely with flesh and blood, but with an evil within us and outside us, which is spirit. Only an evil which attaches to us by our own act, but does so from birth, can therefore be designated as radical evil. And it is noteworthy that Kant, who did not in theory rise to a transcendental act determining all human existence, was led in later investigations by sheer faithful observation of the phenomena of moral judgment, to the recognition of a subjective basis of human conduct (as he expressed it) which preceded every act within the range of the senses, but which, in turn, had itself to be an act of freedom. On the other hand Fichte, who had | speculatively grasped the concept of such an act, reverted in his theory of morals, to the current humanitarianism and was content to find this evil (which precedes all empirical action) only in the inertia of human nature. *389*

There seems to be only one reason that could be raised in objection to this view: namely that it cuts out all conversions from good to evil and *vice versa* for man, at least in this life. However if it happens that human or divine aid—for some aid man always needs—determines him to change his conduct to the good, the fact that man accepts this influence of the good, and does not positively shut it out from him,—this fact is also to be found in that initial act because of which he is this individual and not another. In the man in whom this transmutation has not yet taken place but in whom, too, the good principle has not completely died, there is that inner voice of his own better self, (better in respect to himself as he now is). It never ceases to urge him to accomplish this transmutation, and as he only finds peace in his inner self through a real and decisive change, he becomes reconciled with his guardian spirit as though the original idea had only now been satisfied. In the strictest sense it is true that, however man be constituted, it is not he himself but either the good or the evil spirit which acts in him, and nevertheless this does no violence to freedom. For this very letting-act-in-him of the good or evil principle is the consequence of the intelligible deed, through which man's being and life are determined.[a]

Having thus presented the origin and development of evil up to its realization in the individual human being, nothing then seems to remain except to describe its manifestation in man.

The general possibility of evil, as has been shown, consists in the fact that, instead of keeping his selfhood as the basis or the instrument, man can strive to elevate it to be the ruling and universal will, and, on the contrary, try to make what is spiritual in him into a means. If in a man the dark principle of selfhood and self-will is completely penetrated by light and is one with it, then God, as | eternal love or as really existent, is the nexus of the forces in him. But if the two principles are at strife, then another spirit occupies the place where God should be. This, namely, is the reverse of God, a being which was roused to actualization by God's revelation but which can never attain to actuality from potentiality, a being which indeed never exists but always wishes to be, and which, like the 'matter' of the ancients, can thus never be grasped as real (actualized) by perfect reason but only by false imagination (λογισμῷ νόθῳ)[1] which is exactly what sin is. Wherefore, since it itself is not real, it takes on the appearance

390

[1] The Platonic expression in the *Timaeus*,[a] page 349, Vol. IX of the Zweibrücken edition; previously in *Tim. Locr. De an. mundi, ibid.* page 5.

of true being in mirrored images, as the serpent borrows colors from light, and strives to lead man to folly in which alone it can be accepted and grasped by him. It is therefore rightly represented not only as the enemy of all creation (because this can only endure through the nexus of love) and especially as the enemy of man, but also as man's tempter who entices him into false pleasures and to the reception of non-being into his imagination. In this it is supported by man's own evil inclinations, for his eye, which is incapable of looking constantly at the glamor of divinity and truth, always gazes at non-being. So the beginning of sin consists in man's going over from actual being to non-being, from truth to falsehood, from light into darkness, in order himself to become the creative basis and to rule over all things with the power of the center which he contains. For even he who has moved out of the center retains the feeling that he has been all things when in and with God. Therefore he strives to return to this condition, but he does so for himself and not in the way he could, that is, in God. Hence there springs the hunger of selfishness which, in the measure that it deserts totality and unity becomes ever needier and poorer, but just on that account more ravenous, hungrier, more poisonous. In evil there is that contradiction which devours and always negates itself, | which just while striving to become creature destroys the nexus of creation and, in its ambition to be everything, falls into non-being. Moreover, manifest sin, unlike mere weakness or impotence, does not fill us with pity but with fear and horror, a feeling which can only be explained by the fact that sin strives to break the Word, to touch the basis of creation and profane the mystery. But even sin should become manifest, for only in contrast to sin is there revealed the

391

innermost tie of dependence of all things, and the essence of God which, as it were, was there *before* all existence (not yet mitigated by it) and therefore terrible. For God himself clothes this principle in creation and covers it with love, in that he makes it the basis and, as it were, the bearer of creatures. Now if someone rouses it through the abuse of self-will which has been raised to self-sufficiency, it becomes actual for him and works against him. For since God cannot, after all, be disturbed in his existence, and, still less, dismissed, therefore in accordance with the necessary correspondence which pertains between God and his basis, the very light of life which shines in the depths of darkness in every single man is fanned in the sinner into a consuming fire. It is the same as when, in a living organism, as soon as a single member organ or system is out of accord with the whole, it feels the very unity and collaboration to which it has opposed itself as fire (= fever) and is inflamed by inner heat.

We have seen how the spirit of man lays itself open to the spirit of lies and falsehood through false imagination and learning oriented towards non-being, and soon fascinated by it, is deprived of its initial freedom. From this it follows that, by contrast, the truly good can only be affected by a divine magic, that is by the immediate presence of being in consciousness and reason. Arbitrary good is as impossible as arbitrary evil. True freedom is in accord with a holy necessity, of a sort which we feel in essential knowledge when heart and spirit, bound only by their own | law, freely affirm that which is necessary. If evil consists in strife between the two principles, then the good can only consist in their complete accord. And the tie which unites the two must be divine, since they are one not in a conditional way but completely and unconditional-

392

ally. The relation of the two is not to be conceived as optional morality or one derived from self-determination. The last concept presupposed that they were not, in themselves, one; but how can they become one if they are not? Besides it leads back to the inconsistent system of the equilibrium of choices. The relation of the two principles is that the dark principle (selfhood) is bound to the light. We may be permitted to express this as religiosity, in the original sense of the word. By this we do not mean what an ailing age calls religiosity—idle brooding, pietistic intimations, or will-to-feel divinity.[a] For God is in us clear knowledge and spiritual light itself. In this alone, far from its being unclear itself, all else becomes clear. And this knowledge does not permit him who has it to be idle or sanctimonious. Wherever it is real, religiosity is something far more substantial than our philosophers-of-feeling opine. We understand religiosity in the original, practical meaning of the word.[b] It is conscientiousness, or acting in accordance with one's knowledge, and not acting contrary to the light of understanding. A man to whom this latter is impossible, not in a human, physical or psychological way but in a divine way, one calls religious, conscientious in the highest sense of the word. He is not conscientious who, in a given case, must first hold the command of duty before himself in order to decide to do right because of his respect for it. By the very meaning of the word, religiosity allows no choice between alternatives, no *aequilibrium arbitrii* (the bane of all morality) but only the highest commitment to the right, without any choice. Conscientiousness does not necessarily and always appear as enthusiasm or extraordinary elevation, although | when the illusion of an optional morality has been laid low, another and even worse spirit of pride would *393* like to have it so. Conscientiousness may appear quite formally, in strict performance of duty, in which case the qualities even of severity and harshness are mixed with it. Thus it was in the soul of Cato, to whom an ancient writer ascribes such an inward and almost divine necessity of action, in saying that he was most like virtue, in that he never did what was right in order to do so (out of respect for the command of duty) but because he simply could not have done otherwise. This severity of attitude, like the severity of life in nature, is the seed out of which alone true comeliness and godlikeness blossom; but the supposedly superior morality,[a] which thinks that it can despise this kernel, is like a sterile blossom, incapable of bringing forth fruit.[1] The highest, just because it is the highest, does not always and everywhere obtain. And anyone will hesitate to declare it to be so who has come to know the breed of spiritual libertines who use just what is highest in science and in sentiment for the crassest spiritual improprieties and superciliousness toward the so-called common sense of duty. It can already be anticipated that on the road on which everyone would rather be a precious spirit than a reasonable one, and would rather be called noble than be just, we will arrive at a point at which ethics will be grounded on the general concept of 'taste,' and wickedness, accordingly, will only consist of a poor or corrupt taste.[2] If the divine principle

[1] Very correct comments on this morality of the superior soul in this age are contained in the review I have frequently cited, by Mr. Friedrich Schlegel in the *Heidelberg Annuals*, page 154.

[2] A young man who, like many other contemporaries, is probably too proud to walk along the honest path of Kant, and who is nonetheless incapable of raising himself to a better view, talks aesthetic nonsense and has already announced such an Ethics based on aesthetics. With such progress, the Kantian jest that Euclid might be considered a somewhat ponderous approach to the art of drawing, may perhaps still become serious too.

of morality itself pulses through a serious disposition, then virtue appears as enthusiasm—as | heroism (in the battle against evil), as the splendid, free courage of a man to act as the god bids him and not to be inferior in action to that which he has recognized in knowledge. It would appear as faith, not in the sense of an ostensibly commendable assuming of something to be true, or as something less than certainty—a meaning which has been attached to this word, by its being used for common things—but in its original meaning, as trust, confidence in what is divine, which excludes all choice. If, finally, a ray of divine love is cast into the inviolable seriousness of purpose which is always presupposed, then the highest transfiguration of the moral life occurs in loveliness and divine beauty.[a]

394

We have now inquired as far as possible into the origin of the contrast between good and evil and into the manner in which the two function together in creation, but the chief problem of this whole inquiry is still ahead of us. Up to now God has merely been viewed as Being revealing itself. But what is his relation as a moral being to this revelation? Is the revelation an activity occurring with blind and unconscious necessity, or is it a free and conscious act? And if it is the latter, what is God's relation as a moral being to evil, the possibility and reality of which depend upon his self-revelation? If he willed this did he also will evil, and how is this willing to be reconciled with his holiness and supreme perfection, or—in the common expression—how is God to be justified in view of evil?

The preliminary question concerning God's freedom in self-revelation seems indeed to have been decided by the foregoing. If God were a mere logical abstraction to us, then everything would have to proceed from him with logical necessity; he himself would be, as it were, only the Supreme Law whence all would derive, but without personality or consciousness thereof. However we have explained God as the living unity of forces; and if personality consists, in accordance with our earlier explanation, in the connection of an autonomous being with a basis which is independent of it, in such a way namely that these two completely | interpenetrate one another and are but one being, then God is the highest personality by reason of the connection of the ideal principle within him to the independent basis (independent relative to the ideal principle)—since the basis and the existent entity in him necessarily unite to become one absolute existence. Moreover if the living unity of the two is spirit, then God as their absolute nexus is spirit in the most eminent and absolute sense. It is also certain that God's personality can only be based upon the nexus between him and nature, as the God of pure idealism as well as the God of pure realism is, by contrast, necessarily an impersonal Being, for which the Fichtean and Spinozistic conceptions are the clearest evidence. However because there is in God an independent basis of reality, and hence two equally eternal beginnings of self-revelation, therefore God with respect to his freedom, must also be viewed in relation to both. The first beginning of creation is the longing of the One to give birth to itself, or the will of the depths. The second is the will of love through which the Word is pronounced in nature and through which God first makes himself personal. The will of the depths can therefore not be free in the sense in which the will of love is. It is not a conscious will, connected with reflection, but neither is it completely lacking in consciousness, moving in accordance

395

with blind, mechanical necessity. But it is of a middle nature, like desire or passion, and most readily comparable to the lovely urge of a developing being striving to unfold itself, whose inner actions are undeliberate (cannot be avoided) and yet involve no sense of compulsion. But the will of love, just because it is this, is altogether free and conscious; the revelation which comes from it is action and deed. All nature tells us that it is in no wise the product of mere geometric necessity; not sheer, pure reason, but personality and spirit are in it (just as we distinguish the reasonable from the creative author). Otherwise geometric reasoning which has ruled so long must long since have fully penetrated nature and have achieved its idol of universal and eternal laws of nature more fully than has yet occurred, | since it must daily rather recognize more fully the irrational relationship between nature and itself. Creation is not an event but an act. There are no consequences of universal laws; but God, that is God's person, is the universal law, and all that happens happens because of God's personality—not on account of an abstract necessity, which in action would be unendurable for *us*, let alone for God. One of the most pleasing aspects of the Leibnizian philosophy, which is all too greatly dominated by the spirit of abstractness, is the recognition that the laws of nature are morally necessary but not mathematically necessary, yet just as little arbitrary. "I have found," says Leibniz, "that the laws which can really be established in nature are nevertheless not absolutely demonstrable, but neither is that necessary. To be sure, they can be proved in several ways, but something must always be presupposed which is not altogether necessary mathematically. Therefore these laws are the proof of a supreme, intelligent and free Being, against the system of absolute necessity. They are neither

396

altogether necessary (in the abstract sense) nor entirely arbitrary, but they stand in between, as laws derived from a wisdom perfect beyond all else."[1] The supreme aim of the dynamic mode of explanation is nothing else than this reduction of the laws of nature to mind, spirit and will.

However, the general recognition of freedom in nature is not sufficient to define the relation of God as a moral being, to the world; in addition the question remains whether the act of self-revelation was free in the sense that all its consequences were foreseen by God. But this too must necessarily be affirmed; for the will to revelation would not be vital if another will, rooted in the inner nature of being, did not stand in contrast to it. Thus in the self-restraint of being, there arises a reflected picture of all which is implicitly contained in being, in which God ideally realizes himself or, what is the same, recognizes

397 himself | in advance of his realization. Thus, since there is in God a tendency working against the will to revelation, love and goodness, or the *communicativum sui,* must predominate in order that there may be a revelation,—and it is this decision which alone really completes the concept of revelation as a conscious and morally free act.

Irrespective of this conception, and though the act of revelation is necessary in God only morally or relative to goodness and love, the notion of a consultation of God with himself, or a choice between various possible worlds, remains an unfounded and untenable one. On the contrary, just as soon as the closer definition of a moral necessity has been added, this proposition is altogether undeniable: that all follows with absolute necessity from God's nature, that all that lies in its power as possible

[1] *Tentam. theod.* Opp. T. I, p. 365, 366.[a]

must also be real, and that anything which is not real must also be morally impossible. Spinozism does not err at all in asserting such an inviolable necessity in God, but only in taking this in a lifeless and impersonal way. For since Spinoza's system in general comprehends only one aspect of the Absolute,—namely the realistic side or the extent to which God operates in the basis,—these propositions do, to be sure, lead to a blind and irrational necessity. But if God is essentially love and goodness, that which is morally necessary in him also follows with a genuinely metaphysical necessity. If perfect freedom in God required choice in the strictest sense, we would then have to go still further. For perfect freedom of choice would only have existed if God could also have created a world less perfect than was possible in accordance with all conditions. Thus some would in turn really assert seriously that, had God so willed, he might have created a better world than this. For there is nothing so inconsistent that it has not at some time or other been brought forward and indeed advanced in full seriousness by some—not merely as in the case of the Castilian King Alfonso whose well known utterance applied only to the Ptolemaic system which then ruled. Thus the reasons against the unity of possibility and actuality | in God are derived from the altogether formal concept of possibility, that all is possible which is not self-contradictory—as, for instance, in the well known objection that all reasonably conceived novels must then be actual occurrences. Even Spinoza had no such merely formal concept; all possibility applies for him only with reference to divine perfection; and Leibniz manifestly accepts this [formal] concept only in order to emphasize a choice in God and to separate himself, in this way, as far as possible from Spinoza. "God chooses between possibili-

398

ties," he says, "and therefore chooses freely without compulsion; only if a single course alone were possible would there be no choice, no freedom." If nothing more were required for freedom than such an empty possibility, then it can be granted that from a formal point of view, without considering the divine essence, there was and still is infinite possibility. However this means that we wish to assert divine freedom by means of a conception which is false in itself and which is possible only in our understanding and not in God whom we can hardly think of as disregarding his essence or his perfection. With regard to the plurality of possible worlds, an unruly matter, still unformed but capable of all forms (such as the original motion of the depths, as we explained) does indeed seem to offer an infinity of possibilities. And if the possibility of several worlds were, perchance, to be founded on this, it would only need to be remarked that, nevertheless, no such possibility would follow with respect to God, since the depths are not to be called God, and God being perfect can only will one course. However even that unruliness can in no wise be thought of as though in the depths there were not contained the archetype of the only world possible in accordance with God's essence, which in actual creation is raised from potentiality to actuality simply by means of the separation, regulation of forces and exclusion of the unruly elements which restrict or darken it. But in the divine understanding, as in primeval wisdom in which God realizes himself ideally or as archetype,—just as there is only one God, so there is but one possible world.

399 | In the divine understanding there is a system; God himself, however, is not a system but a life, and this alone constitutes the answer to the question as to the possibility of evil in relation to God—for the sake of which the foregoing was considered. All existence must be conditioned in order that it may be actual, that is, personal, existence. God's existence, too, could not be personal if it were not conditioned, except that he has the conditioning factor *within* himself and not outside himself. He cannot set aside the condition, for if he did he would have to set aside himself; he can only subdue it through love and subordinate it to him for his glorification. In God, too, there would be a depth of darkness if he did not make the condition his own and unite it to him as one and as absolute personality. Man never gains control over the condition even though in evil he strives to do so; it is only loaned to him independent of him; hence his personality and selfhood can never be raised to complete actuality. This is the sadness which adheres to all finite life, and inasmuch as there is even in God himself a condition at least relatively independent, there is in him, too, a source of sadness which, however, never attains actuality but rather serves for the eternal joy of triumph. Thence the veil of sadness which is spread over all nature, the deep, unappeasable melancholy of all life. Joy must have sorrow, sorrow must be transfigured in joy. Thus that which comes from mere conditioning or from the depths, does not come from God, even though it is necessary for his existence. But it cannot be said either, that evil comes from the depths or that the will of the depths is its primal cause. For evil can only arise in the innermost will of one's own heart, and is never achieved without one's own deed. The solicitation of the depths, or the reaction against what is above the creature, only awakens the creature passions or the individual will, but it awakens this only so that an independent basis for the good may be there and so that it may be conquered and penetrated by the good. For aroused selfhood is not in

400 itself evil but only insofar as it has totally | torn itself asunder from its opposite, light or the universal will. Only this very rejection of the good is sin. Activated selfhood is necessary for life's intensity;[a] without it there would be complete death, goodness slumbering; for where there is no battle there is no life. The will of the depths is therefore only the awakening of life, not evil immediately and for itself. If the will of man envelops activated selfhood with love, and subordinates it to light as the universal will, then for the first time goodness awakens and becomes actual in man through the intensity inherent in universal will. Thus in the good the reaction of the depths works towards goodness, in the bad it works towards evil—as Scripture says: in the pious thou art pious; in the perverse, perverse.[b] Goodness without effective selfhood is itself an ineffective goodness. The same thing which becomes evil through creature-will (if it isolates itself completely, to exist for itself) is in itself good, so long, that is, as it remains enwrapped in goodness and in the depths. Only selfhood which has been overcome, that means brought back from activity to potentiality,[c] is good; and as potential, having been overcome by the good it remains evermore in the good. If there were in the body no source of coldness, warmth could not be felt. It is impossible to think of an attracting or a repelling force in itself, for on what can the repelling force operate if the attracting one does not give it an object, or on what can attraction operate if it does not contain within it a repellant? Hence it is quite correct to say dialectically: Good and evil are the same, only regarded from different aspects; or evil in itself, that is regarded at the root of its identity, is goodness; just as goodness, on the other hand, regarded in its division or non-identity, is evil. For this reason the state-

ment is also quite correct that whoever has no material or force for evil in himself is also impotent for good, of which we have seen sufficient examples in our time. The passions against which our negative morality is at war are forces each of which has | a common root with its corresponding virtue. The soul of all hatred is love, and in the most violent anger there is seen nothing but the quietude which was attacked and aroused in the innermost center. In their proper measure and organic equilibrium the passions are the very strength of virtue itself and its immediate tools. "If the passions are the limbs of dishonor," says the excellent J. G. Hamann,[a] "do they therefore cease to be the weapons of manhood? Do you understand the alphabet of reason more wisely than the allegorist chamberlain of the Alexandrian Church understood Scripture, when he castrated himself for the sake of the Kingdom of Heaven? The prince of this aeon makes those who do themselves most harm his favorites—his (the devil's) court jesters and fools are the worst enemies of fair nature, which indeed has the corybants and Galli as its gluttonous priests, but strong spirits as its true devotees."[1] Only one would wish that those whose philosophy is more appropriate for a lady's boudoir than for the Academy or palaestra of the Lyceum, would not present the above dialectical propositions to a public which misunderstands them as much as they themselves do, and sees therein a setting aside of all differences between right and wrong, good and evil. Such statements are as inappropriate for this audience as the propositions of the ancient dialecticians, Zeno and the other Eleatics, for a forum of shallow *Precieux*.

401

Self-will is aroused only in order that love in man

[1] *Cloverleaf of hellenistic Letters,* II, page 196.[b]

may find a material or contrast in which to realize itself. To the extent to which selfhood in its apostasy is the principle of evil, the depths do indeed arouse the possible principle of evil, but not evil itself or for the sake of evil. But even this incitement of self-will does not occur in accordance with God's free will, for God does not move in the depths in accordance with this nor from his heart, but only according to his attributes.

Therefore, whoever should assert that God himself willed evil would have to look for the basis of this assertion in the act of self-revelation as creation, just as it has often been thought that he | who willed the world also had to will evil. However in the fact that God brought the disorderly spawn of chaos into order and pronounced his eternal unity in nature, he really opposed darkness and set up the Word as a constant center and eternal beacon against the unruly movement of the irrational principle. The will to creation was thus directly only a will to bring light to birth and, therein, goodness. Evil, however, did not come into consideration for this will, either as a means or, as Leibniz says, as a *conditio sine qua non* of the greatest possible perfection of the world.[1] It was neither the object of a divine decree, nor—and still less—of a permission. But the question why God did not prefer not to reveal

402

[1] *Tentam, theod.* p. 139: Ex his concludendum est. Deum *antecedenter* velle omne *bonum in se*, velle consequenter *optimum* tanquam *finem;* indifferens et malum physicum tanquam *medium;* sed velle tantum *permittere* malum morale, tanquam *conditionem, sine qua non* obtineretur optimum, ita nimirum, ut malum nonnisi titulo necessitatis hypotheticae, id ipsum cum optimo connectentis, admittatur.—p. 292: Quod ad vitium attinet, superius ostensum est, illud non esse objectum decreti divini, *tanquam medium,* sed tanquam *conditionem sine qua non*—et ideo duntaxat *permitti.*—These two passages contain the germ of the entire Leibnizian Theodicy.[a]

himself at all, since he necessarily foresaw that evil would at least follow as an accompaniment of Self-revelation, this question really deserves no reply. For this would be as much as saying that love itself should not be, so that there could be no contrast to love; that is, the absolutely positive should be sacrificed to that which has its existence only as a contrast; the eternal should be sacrificed to the merely temporal. We have already explained that God's self-revelation should be regarded not as an unconditioned, arbitrary act, but as an act morally necessary, in which love and goodness triumphed over absolute inwardness. Thus if God had not revealed himself on account of evil, evil would have been victorious over goodness and love. The Leibnizian concept of evil as a *conditio sine qua non,* can | only refer to the basis, inasmuch as this aroused creature-will (the possible principle of evil) is the condition upon which alone the will of love could be realized. We have, moreover, shown before why God does not oppose this will of the depths or set it aside. This would be just as though God set aside the condition of his existence, that is, his own personality. Thus, in order that evil should not be, God himself would have not to be.

403

Another objection, which applies however not merely against this view but against all metaphysics, is the following: that even if God did not will evil he nevertheless continues to be effective in every sinner and gives him the force to accomplish evil. Now this must be admitted altogether, but with an appropriate reservation. The primal basis of existence does continue to be effective in evil, as health continues to be effective in disease, and even the most broken down, counterfeit life remains in God and moves in him insofar as he is the basis of existence. But it feels him as being consuming wrath, and is driven by the attraction of the depths themselves to ever increasing tension against unity, until it comes to self-destruction and final crisis.

After all this, the question ever remains: does evil end, and how? Has creation a final purpose at all, and if so why is it not attained immediately, why does perfection not exist from the very beginning? There is no answer to this except the one already given: because God is a life, not a mere being. All life has a destiny and is subject to suffering and development. God freely submitted himself to this too, in the very beginning, when, in order to become personal, he divided light and the world of darkness. For being is only aware of itself in becoming. To be sure, there is in being no becoming; in the latter, being is itself rather posited as in eternity; but in actualization, there is necessarily a becoming. All history remains incomprehensible without the concept of a humanly suffering God, a concept which is common to all the mysteries and spiritual religions of ancient times. Scripture, too, | distinguishes periods of revelation,[a] and puts that time into a distant future when God will be all in all, that is, when he will be completely realized. The first period of creation, as has previously been shown, is the birth of light. Light, or the ideal principle, as an eternal contrast to the dark principle, is the creative Word which redeems the hidden life in the depths from non-being, raises it from potency to actuality. Spirit rises above the Word and is the first being which unites the dark world and the world of light and subordinates both principles to it for the sake of realization and personality. However, the depths react to this unity and maintain the original duality, but only for ever increasing intensification and for the final division of good and evil. The will of the depths must abide in

404

its freedom till all has been fulfilled, till all has become real. If it were conquered sooner, the good would remain concealed in it together with evil. But the good is to be raised out of darkness to actuality in order to dwell with God everlastingly; and evil is to be separated from goodness in order to be cast out eternally into non-being. For this is the final purpose of creation, that that which could not be in itself, shall be in itself through being raised out of darkness as a depth independent of God, and elevated into existence. Hence the necessity of birth and of death. God yields the ideas which were in him without independent life, to selfhood and non-being, so that in being called from this into life, they may again be in him as independent entities.[1] Thus in its freedom the basis effects the separation and the judgment (κρίσις) and in this very way accomplishes God's complete actualization. For if evil is altogether separated from the good it also ceases to *be* as evil. It could only be effective through misused goodness which was in it without its being conscious of it. In life it still enjoyed the forces of external nature with which it attempted to be creative, and it still had an | indirect share in God's goodness. But in death it is separated from all goodness, and indeed it remains as desire, as the eternal hunger and thirst for reality, but is unable to go beyond potentiality. Its condition is therefore a state of non-being, a state of constant consumption of activity or of that which strives to be active in it. The reconstruction of evil into goodness (the return of all things) is therefore in nowise required for the realization of the ideal of a final, inclusive perfection; for evil is bad only insofar as it goes beyond potentiality; but when reduced to non-

405

[1] *Philosophy and Religion*, (Tübingen, 1804) Page 73.[b]

being, or the state of potentiality, it is as it always should be, a basis, subjected, and as such no longer in contradiction to God's holiness or love. The end of revelation is therefore the banishment of evil from the good, its exposure as being altogether unreal. On the other hand, the good which has been raised from the depths is combined in everlasting unity with the original good; those who have been born out of darkness into light join the ideal principle as members of its body in which there is the perfectly realized being, now altogether personal. As long as the initial duality persisted, the creative Word ruled in the depths, and this period of creation endures throughout all until the end. But if the duality is destroyed by separation, the Word, or the ideal principle, subordinates itself to spirit, together with the real principle which has thus become one with it; and spirit, as divine consciousness, lives equally in both principles. As Scripture says of Christ: He must rule until all his enemies lie underfoot.[a] The last enemy which is transcended is death[b] (for death was necessary only for the separation; the good must die in order to be separated from evil, and the evil in order to be separated from goodness). But if all will have become subject to him, then the Son himself shall also be subjected to him that did subject all things unto him, that God may be all in all.[c] For not even spirit itself is supreme; it is

406 but spirit, or the breath | of love. But love is supreme. It is that which was before there were the depths and before existence (as separate entities), but it was not there as love, rather—how shall we designate it?

Here at last we reach the highest point of the whole inquiry. The question has long been heard: What is to be gained by that initial distinction between being insofar as it is basis, and being insofar as it exists? For either there is no common ground for the two—in which case we must declare ourselves in favor of absolute dualism; or there is such common ground—and in that case, in the last analysis, the two coincide again. In that case we have one being in all opposites, an absolute identity of light and darkness, good and evil, and all the inconsistent consequences which must befall any intellectualistic system and of which this system too, has indeed been accused for quite some time.

We have already explained what we assume in the first respect: there must be a being *before* all basis and before all existence, that is, before any duality at all; how can we designate it except as 'primal ground' or, rather, as the 'groundless'? As it precedes all antitheses these cannot be distinguishable in it or be present in any way at all. It cannot then be called the identity of both, but only the absolute indifference as to both. Most people, when they reach a point of view at which they must recognize the disappearance of all antitheses, forget that these have now really disappeared, and predicate the same distinctions of the indifference which, however, arose precisely through their total cessation. Indifference is not a product of antitheses, nor are they implicitly contained in it, but it is a unique being, apart from all antitheses, in which all distinctions break up. It is naught else than just their non-being, and therefore has no predicates except lack of predicates, without its being naught or a non-entity. Thus they must either really posit indifference in the 'groundless,' which precedes all basis; and then they have | neither good nor evil—(for we leave, for the time being, as self-evident the fact that the erection of a distinction between good and evil is, from this standpoint, altogether inadmissible)—and in this event they can predicate of the

407

groundless neither one nor the other, nor both at the same time. Or, if they posit good and evil, then they at once posit duality, and thus no longer have the groundless or indifference. The following may be said for the explication of the last point: Reality and ideality, darkness and light, or however else we wish to designate the two principles, can never be predicated of the groundless *as antitheses.* But nothing prevents their being predicated as non-antitheses, that is, in disjunction and each *for itself;* wherein, however, this duality (the real twofoldness of the principles) is established. There is in the groundless itself nothing to prevent this. For just because its relation towards both is a relation of total indifference, it is neutral towards both. If it were the absolute identity of both, it could only be both *at the same time;* that is, both would have to be predicated of it as *antitheses,* and hence would themselves again be one. Thus out of this neither-nor, or out of indifference, duality immediately breaks forth (which is something quite different from opposition, even though we may have used the two as meaning the same thing up to the present, as we had not yet arrived at this point in the inquiry)—and *without* indifference, that is, *without* the groundless, there would be no twofoldness of the principles. Instead of undoing the distinction, as was expected, the groundless rather posits and confirms it. Far from the distinction between the basis and existence[a] being merely a logical one, introduced only as a makeshift and to be found spurious again in the end, it showed itself rather to be a very real distinction which was only rightly valued and fully comprehended from the highest standpoint.

After this dialectical exposition we can now explain ourselves altogether definitely in the following way. The essence of the basis, or of existence, can only be precedent to all basis, | that is, the absolute viewed directly, the groundless. But, as has been shown, it cannot be this in any other way than by dividing into two equally eternal beginnings, not that it is both *at the same time* but that it is in both *in the same way,* as the whole in each, or a unique essence. But the groundless divides itself into the two equally eternal beginnings only in order that the two which could not be in it as groundless at the same time, or there be one, should become one through love; that is, it divides itself only that there may be life and love and personal existence. For there is love neither in indifference nor where antitheses are combined which require the combination in order to be; but rather (to repeat a word which has already been spoken) this is the secret of love, that it unites such beings as could each exist in itself, and nonetheless neither is nor can be without the other.[1] Therefore, as duality comes to be in the groundless, there also comes to be love, which combines the existent (ideal) with the basis of existence. But the basis remains free and independent of the Word until the final, complete separation. Then it dissolves as in man, when he is converted to clarity and establishes himself as an enduring being, the initial longing is dissolved, in that all that is true and good in it is elevated into clear consciousness, while all the rest, namely what is false and impure, is eternally sealed in darkness to remain as the eternally dark depths of selfhood, as the *caput mortuum* of his life process, and as potentiality which can never advance to actuality. Then all is subordinated to spirit; in spirit existence is one with the basis of existence; in it both really are at the same

408

[1] *Aphorisms on the Philosophy of Nature* in the *Annuals of Medicine as a Science.* Volume I, No. 1. aphorisms 162, 163.[a]

time, or it is the absolute identity of the two. But beyond the spirit is the initial 'groundless' which is no longer indifference (neutrality) but nonetheless not the identity of the two principles but rather the general unity, the same towards all but still not partisan to anything. It is now a beneficence which is free from all and which nonetheless works through all,—in a word, it is love which is all in all.

409 | Thus he would be quite right who wished to say, (as before): In this system there is one principle for everything; it is one and the same being reigning in the dark depths of nature and in eternal clarity, one and the same effecting the severity and isolation of things, and unity and kindness, the same thing that rules with the will of love in goodness and with the will of anger in evil. But although he would be quite right in saying this, he should not forget the following: that the one being really divides itself into two beings in its two functions, that in the one it is *only* the basis of existence, in the other only essence (and therefore only ideal); moreover that only God as spirit is the absolute identity of both principles, but only because and insofar as both are *subjected* to his personality. But whoever found in this final, highest viewpoint an absolute identity of good and evil, would show his total ignorance, since evil and good in no way form an original antithesis, least of all a duality. There is a duality when there are really two beings which stand in opposition to one another. Evil, however, is no being but a counterfeit of being, which is real only by contrast, not in itself. Moreover, absolute identity, the spirit of love, is prior to evil just because the latter can only appear in contrast to it. Hence, too, it cannot be comprehended in absolute identity, but is rather excluded and banished from it

eternally.[1]

Finally, since all antitheses disappear with respect to the Absolute when regarded as such, whoever wishes to call this system pantheism should have this privilege too.[2] We gladly grant | everyone his own manner of making intelligible to himself the age and what is contained in it. The name does not matter; what counts is the substance. *410*

[1] From this it is clear how strange is the demand that the distinction of good and evil should be explained at once in the first principles. Whoever considers good and evil a real duality and regards dualism as the most perfect system, must indeed talk like that.

[2] No one can join more heartily that the author in the wish expressed by Mr. Friedrich Schlegel in the *Heidelberg Annuals,* No. 2, page 242,[a] that the unmanly pantheistic bunkum might cease in Germany, particularly as he also adds the aesthetic delusions and conceits, and | we, furthermore, may also count the opinion as to the exclusive reasonableness of Spinozism as part of this bunkum. It is, to be sure, very easy in Germany to start a false or even a fake doctrine going, where philosophic system-making is such a literary industry, and so many to whom nature denied intelligence for even everyday affairs believe themselves called upon to join in philosophizing. One can at least be comforted by the consciousness of never having favored it personally nor encouraged it by one's own helpful support, but of being able to say with Erasmus (however little one may otherwise have in common with him): *Semper solus esse volui nihilque peius odi quam iuratus et factiosos.* The author never desired through founding a sect to take away from others and least of all from himself, the freedom of inquiry in which he has always declared himself and presumably always will declare himself to be engaged. In the future, too, he will retain the procedure which he followed in the present treatise, where, even though the form of a dialogue is lacking, everything is nonetheless developed as in a dialogue. Many things could have been defined more precisely and kept less informal; many things could more expressly have been saved from misinterpretation. The author failed to do so in part purposely. Whoever cannot accept it from him in this way, or does not wish to, had better take nothing from him at all and seek other sources. But perhaps self-appointed followers and opponents may grant this treatise the respect which they bestowed on the earlier, related essay, *Philosophy and Religion,* by ignoring it altogether, to which course the former were certainly led less by the threats in the preface or by the manner of presentation than by the content itself. *410n*

In the introduction to this treatise we already touched on the vanity of a polemic such as uses the more general concepts of philosophic systems against a particular one which may well have some common points of contact with them and hence has already been confused with all of them, but which has its unique characteristics at every single point. Thus it can glibly be said that a system teaches the immanence of things in God; but nonetheless with respect to ourselves, for instance, this would mean nothing, even though it could not exactly be called untrue. For we have sufficiently shown that all natural creatures have a mere being in the depths or in the initial longing which has not yet achieved unity with understanding, that they are thus mere peripheral | entities in relation to God. *411* Only man is in God, and through this very being-in-God is capable of freedom. He alone is a central being and therefore should also remain in the center. In him all things are created, just as it is also only through man that God accepts nature and ties it to him. Nature is the first, or old, Testament, since things are still outside the center and therefore under the law. Man is the beginning of the new covenant through whom, as mediator, since he himself is connected with God, God (the last division being attained) also accepts nature and takes it to *him*. Man is thus the redeemer of nature[a] towards whom all its archetypes strive. The Word which is fulfilled in man exists in nature as a dark, prophetic (still incompletely spoken) Word. Hence the anticipations which have no exegesis in nature itself and are only explained by man. Hence the general purposiveness of causes which likewise becomes intelligible only from this standpoint. Now, whoever omits or overlooks all these qualifications can easily make a refutation. A criticism which concerns historicity alone is indeed an easy one. In it one need not contribute anything of one's own resources and can fittingly observe the precept: *Caute, per Deos! incede, latet ignis sub cinere doloso.* Nevertheless wilful and unproved assumptions are unavoidable. Thus it would require nothing less than the whole power of a deeply pondered and thoroughly developed philosophy to prove that there are only two ways of explaining evil—the dualistic, according to which there is assumed to be an evil basic being, regardless with what modifications, beneath or alongside the good; and the cabbalistic, according to which evil is explained by emanation and withdrawal. It would be necessary to prove this and to show that because of it every other system must annul the difference between good and evil. In a philosophic system every concept has its definite place where alone it is valid and which determines its significance and circumscribes it. Now who can judge the whole who does not penetrate to the inner structure but just lifts the most general conceptions out of their connection? Thus we | exposed the definite point of the system where the concept of indifference is, to be sure, the only possible concept of the Absolute. But if this concept is now taken abstractly, the whole is distorted and one may then infer that this system sets aside the personality of the Supreme Being. We have up to the present remained silent regarding this oft heard accusation as well as many others, but believe that we have established the first distinct conception of that personality in this treatise. In the 'groundless' or the 'indifferent' there is indeed no personality; but is the point of origin the whole? Now we challenge those who so readily made that accusation to present us in turn with anything, however trifling, on this conception, that is intelligible. Instead we find them saying everywhere that God's

412

personality is incomprehensible and in no way to be made intelligible. In this they are quite right, since they regard those abstract systems in which all personality is entirely impossible, as the only ones in accordance with reason. This is presumably also the cause of their ascribing the same view to everyone who does not despise science and reason. We, on the contrary, are of the opinion that a clear, reasonable insight must be possible particularly into the supreme conceptions, since only thereby can they become truly ours, enter into us and be eternally founded. Yes, we go still further and with Lessing regard even the development of the truths of revelation into truths of reason as utterly necessary if the human race is to be helped thereby.[1] Similarly we are convinced that reason is entirely sufficient to expose every possible error (in veritable matters of the spirit) and that the heresy-hunting attitude in judging philosophic systems can altogether be dispensed with.[2] A thoroughly illiberal and highly restrictive point of view is introduced into history by the whole notion that there is an absolute dualism of good and evil running through it in accordance with which either the one or the other principle rules in all the manifestations and works of the human spirit, and according to which there are only two philosophic systems | and two religions, one absolutely good and the other utterly evil. The same over-simplification follows from the opinion that everything began in purity and innocence and that all later developments (which, after all, were necessary in order fully to reveal the partial aspects contained in the first

413

[1] *Education of the Human Race.* § 76.

[2] Particularly if, on the other side, one wishes to talk only about *opinions* when one should speak of Truths by which alone salvation can be secured.

unity, and thereby perfectly to reveal this unity itself) all these later developments were but corruptions and counterfeits.—This whole view may indeed serve in criticism as a mighty sword of Alexander which will everywhere and without trouble strike the Gordian knot in twain, [yet, as was said, it is most illiberal and restrictive]. There was a time which preceded that dualism, and there was a world-view and religion which, though opposed to the absolute one, arose on its own basis and not as a falsification of the first. Taken historically, paganism[a] is as original as Christianity, and even if it is only the foundation and basis of the higher form it is, nonetheless, not derivative.

These considerations lead us back to our point of departure. A system which contradicts the most sacred sentiments and feelings and moral consciousness can, at least in these characteristics, never be called a system of reason, but rather of unreason. On the contrary, a system in which reason fulfilled itself, would have to unite all the demands of the spirit as of the heart, of the most conscientious feeling as of the strictest understanding. The polemic against reason and science does indeed permit a kind of distinguished generality which circumvents precise concepts, so that we can more easily guess its purposes than its exact meaning. Moreover we fear that even if we fathomed it, we would not reach anything extraordinary. For however highly we place reason, we still do not believe, for example, that anyone can through pure reason become virtuous or a hero or any kind of great man, nor even—in the well known phrase—that the human race can be propagated by it. Only in personality is there life; and all personality rests on a dark foundation which must, to be sure, also be the foundation of knowledge. But only reason can

414 bring forth what is contained in these depths, | hidden and merely potential, and elevate it to actuality. This can occur only through distinction, that is through science and dialectic. And we are convinced that they alone will grasp and bring to eternal knowledge that system which has been present more often than we realize, but which has always again escaped, which has hovered before all of us but has never yet been entirely apprehended by anyone. As in life we actually trust only vigorous reason, and miss all true tenderness in those especially who always expose their feelings to our gaze, so too, where we are considering truth and knowledge, selfhood which has merely reached the point of feelings cannot win our confidence. The emotions are glorious when they stay in the depths, but not when they come forth into the day and wish to become of the essence and to rule. If, in accordance with the striking views of Franz Baader, the impulse to know has the closest analogy to the procreative impulse,[1] so is there in knowledge, too, something analogous to modesty and shame, and on the other hand, also an immodesty and shamelessness, a kind of faun-like passion which samples all things without serious purpose and without the love of really producing or creating anything. The nexus of our personality is the spirit, and if the active combination of both principles can alone be creative and productive, then inspiration in the actual sense is the effective principle of every productive or creative art or science. Every inspiration expresses itself in a definite way; and thus there is one which expresses itself in the impulse of dialectic art, a really scientific inspiration. Hence there is also a dialectical philosophy which as a science is certainly distinct from poetry and

[1] *Cf.* his treatise on the above subject in the *Annuals for Medicine,* Vol. III, No. 1, p. 113.[a]

religion, for instance; and which is something all by itself, not identical with all possible things one after another, as those assert who are at present endeavoring to confuse everything with everything else in so many writings. It is said that reflection is in enmity against ideas; but it is just the supreme triumph of Truth that it can come forth victorious from the most extreme division | and analysis. *415* Reason is in man what, according to the mystics, the *primum passivum* is in God, or initial wisdom in which all things are together and yet severred, at one and yet each in its way free. It is not activity as spirit, not absolute identity of both principles of knowledge, but rather indifference, the measure and, as it were, the universal locus of Truth, the quiet abode wherein original wisdom is conceived, towards which the understanding should work as in beholding its archetype. Philosophy takes its name, on the one hand, from love, as the universally inspiring principle, and on the other, from this original wisdom which is its actual goal.[a]

If the dialectical principle (that is understanding, which divides but on this very account arranges and shapes things organically) as well as the archetype towards which it is directed, are withdrawn from philosophy at the same time, so that it no longer has either measure or rule in itself, then, to be sure, it has no other way than to strive to orientate itself historically and to take as its source and guiding principle the *tradition* to which it was referred earlier with similar results.[b] Then it is time to seek for philosophy, too, an historical standard and foundation, just as it was intended to establish poetry among us through a study of the writings of all nations.[c] We entertain the greatest respect for the profound significance of historical investigations, and believe that we have shown that we do not share the *almost* universal opinion that man only gradually raised himself from the stupor of animal instinct to reason. Nevertheless we believe that Truth lies nearer to us and that we should first seek the solution for the problems which have become vital in our time, among ourselves and on our own soil, before we wander to such distant sources. The time of merely historical faith is past, as soon as the possibility of immediate knowledge is given. We have an earlier revelation than any written one—nature. It contains archetypes which no one has yet interpreted, whereas the written ones have long since re-

416 ceived their fulfillment and exegesis. | If the understanding of that unwritten revelation were inaugurated, the only true system of religion and science would appear, not in the miserable garb pieced together out of a few philosophical and critical conceptions, but at once in the full significance of truth and of nature. Now is not the time to reawaken old quarrels but to seek that which lies beyond and above all factions.

The present treatise will be followed by a series of others in which that part of philosophy which deals with the ideal will gradually be disclosed as a whole.[a]

NOTES ON THE TRANSLATION

These notes are grouped with reference to Schelling's Works, VII, pp. 333-416, the pagination of which is indicated in the margins of the translation.

333 [a] The "Philosophical Inquiries into the Nature of Human Freedom and Matters connected therewith" first appeared in a volume of essays published by Schelling in 1809 entitled "Philosophical Writings, Volume I." (*F. W. J. Schellings philosophische Schriften. Erster Band.* Landshut bei Philipp Krüll, Universitätsbuchhändler, 1809). In this volume, evidently intended as the first of a series of collected works, the Inquiries appeared as the fifth and last essay, pp. 397-511, and the prefatory comment on pp. vii-xii of Schelling's introduction. Cf. Bibliography, below.

[b] The marginal pagination refers to the collected edition of Schelling's works edited by his son K. F. A. Schelling (*Friedrich Wilhelm Joseph von Schellings sämmtliche Werke,* Stuttgart und Augsburg, J. G. Cotta'scher Verlag, 1860). In this edition the Inquiries appeared in Volume VII of the first division, pp. 331-416. In these Notes all references to Schelling's Works are made to this edition.

[c] This "general presentation of his system" was published in 1801 in the "Journal for Speculative Physics" (*Zeitschrift für spekulative Physik*). Under the title "Presentation of my System of Philosophy" (*Darstellung meines Systems der Philosophie*) it appeared in Volume II, number 2, pp. 1-127 of the Journal. Cf. Works IV, pp. 105-212.

334 [a] Cf. Schelling's "Philosophy and Religion" (*Philosophie und Religion,* 1804, Works, VI, pp. 11-70): "The crowd of noisy opponents will at last disperse of its own accord when it becomes aware that it tires itself in vain. It is less to be expected in Germany that the crowd of people will disperse who, without vocation, make them-

selves the uninspired and uninvited adherents of a doctrine. They bear their yoke to the equal amazement of the wise and the impressionable. They are those who are too incompetent to grasp the genuine mysteries of science and who throw themselves at it and stuff it with a mass of strange ideas which they put into it to make a caricature; or they express the truth whose meaning is based on profundities in a few superficial phrases which have no meaning and only astonish the vulgar mob. Or they are those who, misusing language, attire an empty spirit otherwise well intentioned, in such words as have powerfully stirred their weak imagination. For above all Germans are prone to enthusiasm, resembling the sexless bees, though only therein, since they industriously seek to carry away and rework that which blossoms and is produced independently of them." Works, VI, pp. 14-15.

335 [a] The translation inadequately gives the sense of Schelling's pun, for in German the word "*Original*" definitely implies eccentricity to an even greater extent than the English "peculiarly original" conveys.

[b] Cf. Schelling's "On the Nature of German Science" (*Über das Wesen deutscher Wissenschaft*, Works, VIII, pp. 1-18): "The German people strives with all its being towards religion but, in accordance with its special character, towards a religion which is combined with understanding and based upon science. Thus Bacon's well known utterance has been verified in a striking way: that philosophy which has been tasted superficially and has only touched the lips leads away from God, but when drained to the bottom leads back to him.

"The rebirth of religion through the highest science, this is really the task of the German spirit, the predetermined goal of all its efforts. Following the necessary period of transition and separation, we take up this work begun by the religious revolution of an earlier century at just the point where it was dropped. Now the age of fulfillment and completion begins." Works, VIII, pp. 8-9.

337 [a] Bracketed words, here and elsewhere, were added by

the translator.

[b] "*abgezogen*" is here interpreted to signify "external," elsewhere in this work, e.g. p. 356, "attenuated" as well as "abstract", e.g. p. 371.

[c] The problem here indicated is the one referred to above, p. 337, line 1; how to reconcile the sense of individual freedom with a systematic world view.

[d] On Schelling's relation to Fichte see Introduction, section II; also Fuchs, *Vom Werden dreier Denker*, pp. 218-219; and Stefansky, *Das hellenisch-deutsche Weltbild*, pp. 83, 125.

338 [a] This work by Friedrich Schlegel (on Schelling's relation to whom see Introduction, section II), "On the Language and Wisdom of the Hindus," (*Über die Sprache und Weisheit der Indier*) appeared in 1808, published by Mohr and Zimmer at Heidelberg. It was republished in Schlegel's collected works (*Friedrich von Schlegels sämmtliche Werke,* Wien, 1846) VIII, pp. 271-382; the following quotation being on pp. 344-345. In the original edition, referred to by Schelling, the following appears on pp. 140-142 at the beginning of chapter V of Book II, "On Pantheism."

"Only one of the oriental systems and points of view which have the greatest historic importance because of their widespread influence, remains to be mentioned: Pantheism. Its spirit is evident in the teaching of the Buddhists, which was introduced into Tibet and China at the time of Christ, about a thousand years after its origin. This teaching holds sway in Siam and the whole Malayan peninsula as well as in Ceylon, and has also spread widely among the peoples of Tartary. At least among the Chinese the doctrine is ascribed to Fo as his genuine, essential and esoteric teaching, the clearest and most definite recognition that All is Naught. This leads naturally to the teaching that All is One. For if in the face of a purely abstract and negative conception of the Infinite, all else has first been destroyed and has vanished, then in the end it itself takes flight and dissolves into nothingness because it was originally empty and without content.

"Nor should it seem strange that we regard this philosophy as the most recent among oriental systems. The historic evidence for this will be adduced below; here we remark only that the deep, living sense of the Infinite and its plenitude of omnipotence must already be very weak and nebulous, before it can dissolve itself into this shadow and hallucination of a One and All which is so hard to distinguish from a Nothingness. All other oriental doctrinal conceptions are still founded upon and refer to divine miracles and revelation, however much all this may be distorted by fable and error. Pantheism is the system of pure reason and thus makes a transition from oriental to European philosophy. It flatters man's self importance as much as it encourages his laziness. When once this great discovery has been made, when once this all-embracing, all-destroying and yet easy scientific and reasonable wisdom has been found, then there is no longer any need for search and exploration.

"All that which others know or believe, which leads in other directions, is error, deception, and weakness of intellect, just as all change and all life is an empty illusion."

340 [a] Cf. II Corinthians 1, 22; 3, 17-18; Acts 17, 28.

[b] Schelling, together with other writers of the Romantic Movement, was largely responsible for reviving interest in and rehabilitating the reputation of Spinoza. As is well known, for over a hundred years after his death, during the period of the so-called Enlightenment, (see Introduction, section II) Spinoza was neglected or, when mentioned at all, was condemned. He was despised by the Deists as an atheist, this "man intoxicated by a sense of God," as Novalis called him. Friedrich Heinrich Jacobi in his "Letters to Moses Mendelssohn" (*Briefe an Moses Mendelssohn,* Berlin, 1785), viewed Spinoza's teaching as the "only consistent system of philosophy" but rejected the doctrine as inconsistent with a belief in God.

Schelling opposed Jacobi and attacked him in the "Inquiries". Jacobi replied in his essay "On Divine Things"

(*Von den göttlichen Dingen,* Leipzig, 1811). Schelling answered this essay in his "Memorandum on Jacobi's Essay on Divine Things and on the Accusation made therein against him of a deliberate, deceptive, lying Atheism." (*Denkmal der Schrift Jacobi's von den göttlichen Dingen und der ihn in derselben gemachten Beschuldigung eines absichtlich täuschenden Lügeredenden Atheismus,* Tübingen, 1812.) Cf. Works, VIII, pp. 19-136.

41 [a] Cf. Schelling's "System of Philosophy as a Whole" (*System der gesammten Philosophie*), Works, VI, pp. 131-576: "One can only call a cause free if its acts according to the Law of Identity by reason of the compulsion of its own essential being without any other determining factor . . . Accordingly a free result is only such a one which follows 1) from the pure essence of the thing, 2) from this in accordance with the Law of Identity." Works, VI pp. 538-9.

42 [a] Karl Leonhard Reinhold (1758-1823) was, after the publication of his "Letters on Kantian Philosophy" (*Briefe über die Kantische Philosophie,* 1786) generally regarded as an outstanding disciple of Kant's. He was a professor of philosophy at Jena, 1786-1794, and then at Kiel. That he was *persona non grata* to Schelling and his friends is evident in correspondence between Schelling and Steffens, and Schelling and August Wilhelm Schlegel as early as 1800. Thus Steffens wrote to Schelling, September 1, 1800 (Letters I, p. 311): "I can forgive Reinhold everything except his pietistic, monkish foxiness . . . You may remember he expressed an unrestrained delight about absolute relativity and relative absoluteness as though this were something which completely floored your philosophy." In December, 1801, Schelling wrote to Schlegel (Letters, I, p. 351): "In the near future I will send you the first number of a 'Critical Journal of Philosophy' which I have undertaken to publish with Hegel. You will find in it, in addition to an introduction on the nature of philosophic criticism in general and its particular relation to the present situation in philosophy, a five or six page long, strong, essay by me about and against Reinhold's stupidities."

[b] Schelling's references to Leibniz are to the Dutens edition of his works, published at Geneva in 1768. He cites Leibniz by referring to the pages of this edition. The translator has, where possible, added the paragraph numbers found uniformly in most editions. Schelling's quotations from Leibniz, like other citations in his writings, are not always exact.

The reference in this note is to the essay (volume I, pp. 11-16): *Responsio ad Objectiones Wissowatii contra Trinitatem e Incarnationem Dei altissimi.*

343 [a] The expression from Spinoza referred to above—p. 340: God is that which etc.

347 [a] "seeing things as dependent"—i.e. seeing them incompletely in contrast to God's complete understanding.

348 [a] F. H. Jacobi, "Letters to Moses Mendelssohn." See above note b to page 340. It is evident from numerous phrases such as "back to the heart" that this entire paragraph is directed against Jacobi and his interpretation of Spinoza.

349 [a] The review here referred to appeared in the "Heidelberg Literary Annuals" (*Heidelberger Jahrbücher der Literatur*) for 1808, volume I, number 1, part 1 devoted to Theology, Philosophy and Pedagogy. The review by Friedrich Schlegel (pp. 129-159) was of Fichte's most recent writings, "On the Character of the Scholar and his Place in the Realm of Freedom," "The Characteristics of the Present Age" and "Directions for the Spiritual Life."

The passage on page 139 to which Schelling refers, reads: "Now if Herr Fichte declares that every pantheistic view can lead to nothing loftier than to such a merely aesthetic religion because the basic idea of pantheism is only relevant and applicable to the world of appearance and fantasy; [if he furthermore declares] that it is a thoroughly objectionable system, which identifies Nature and Divinity in the manner of Spinoza—then all those who had passed beyond the first difficulties of speculation would surely agree with him. If he wished for once to consider the philosophy of the age from this viewpoint then the only essential thing which really mattered was a detailed and thorough scientific refutation of Spinoza, instead of vague accusations. With Spinoza everything which Herr Fichte would like to clear away surely stands or falls."

[b] "The utterance set forth above"—p. 338 footnote.

350 [a] "intensifying"—*potenzierend,* i.e. raising to a higher power.

351 [a] "Idealism (which does not understand itself)"—in the text the parenthesis is not closed until the end of the sentence, evidently a misprint.

[b] "any earlier revolution"—e.g. Kant's "Copernican Revolution." Cf. Introduction, section II.

[c] "a higher realism"—i.e. Schelling's Philosophy of Nature.

354 [a] Concerning Schelling's conception of "Indifference," see below pp. 406, 412, 415.

357 [a] Concerning "individual minds" who anticipated the Philosophy of Nature, Jacob Böhme for instance, see Introduction, section V.

[b] Cf. below, p. 407, for the consequences of the distinction between Being as existence and Being as the basis of existence.

[c] "The Journal for Speculative Physics" (*Zeitschrift für Spekulative Physik*) was edited by Schelling and published by Christian Ernst Gabler at Jena and Leipzig. The references on pp. 357 and 358 of the Inquiries are to volume II, number 2, of the Journal for 1801. The passages referred to on these pages are in Schelling's Works, IV, as follows:

§ 54 note—Works, IV, p. 146
§ 93 note—Works, IV, p. 163
p. 114—Works, IV, 203
pp. 59, 60—Works, IV, p. 163 (but the footnotes do not appear in the Journal.)
p. 41—Works, IV, p. 146
p. 114—Works, IV, p. 203

359 [a] *"das Regellose"* has here, and elsewhere, been trans-

lated: "*the unruly.*" Alternative suggestions: "the normless," "the inchoate."

360 [a] Schelling here uses the term "*Verstand*" which in other passages is translated "understanding" (e.g. p. 359). While the Kantian distinction between "*Verstand*" (understanding) and "*Vernunft*" (reason) may be found relevant in some passages, it does not always seem applicable, and traditional English usage is better served by sometimes translating "*Verstand*" as "reason." In some passages Schelling himself seems to use the terms interchangeably (e.g. pp. 371-372, 374 and 413-414).

361 [a] "*Logogriph,*" a kind of anagram puzzle, corresponds to Schelling's "*Wort des Rätsels,*" an unusual form of "*Rätselwort.*" As Schelling balances "*Wort der Sehnsucht*" with "*Wort des Rätsels,*" the translation suggests a "*logic of longing*" corresponding to the "*logos*" in the "*logograph.*"

[b] "*Ein-bildung,*" here rendered: "*in-vention,*" is a clever, and significant, pun. The German phrase, "*in die Natur hineingebildet,*" has not been linked in the translation to "invention," though the "forms" "conceived in Nature" could be thought of as in a kind of natural "inventory."

362 [a] "*is turned inwards*"—the text reads "*nach ihnen,*" but as this seems to have no antecedent the translation takes it to be a misprint for *nach innen.*

363 [a] Cf. Stuttgart Private Lectures (*Stuttgarter Privatvorlesungen,* 1810, Works, VII, pp. 417-484): "This nexus is very significantly called the Word, a) because in it and only with it all possibility of differentiation arises; b) because in it are organically united self-being and non-being, vowel and consonant (A=vowel, B=consonant, Being which is itself without utterance and which is only elevated to intelligibility through the Ideal or A)." Works VII, p. 442.

364 [a] On "personality" and God see below page 412; also Introduction, section II.

366 [a] Cf. Stuttgart Lectures: "What, for instance, is sickness?

A condition *contrary to nature* and insofar a condition which could not *be* and nonetheless *is,* lacking basic reality and yet again undeniably a fruitful reality. Evil in the moral world is what sickness is in the bodily world; regarded in one aspect it is the most decided non-being, and yet it has terrible reality." Works, VII, pp. 436-437.

[b] Concerning Schelling's relation to Baader, see Introduction section V.

368 [a] Concerning Schelling's references to Leibniz see above note b to page 342. All the references on this page and below, pp. 369, 370, 396, and 402 are to volume I of the Dutens edition, *Tentaminum Theodicaeae, de Bonitate Dei, Libertate Hominis, et Origine Mali,* pp. 117-403. The references on page 368 are: p. 136—§ 20; p. 240—§ 149; p. 387—§ 380.

369 [a] § 153.

370 [a] p. 141, § 30.

[b] "transformation of normal temperature into distemper" —a free rendering of the German: *Temperatur in Distemperatur.*

371 [a] "such ideas" as ours? The German syntax is ambiguous. The phrase may refer to "such ideas" as Plato's or to "such ideas" as Schelling's own.

373 [a] Cf. Stuttgart Lectures: "Hence it is so important to recognize 1) that the body, too, in and of itself already contains a spiritual principle; 2) that it is not the body which infects the spirit, but the spirit the body; the good man kindles the body with the goodness of his spirit, the bad with the evil of his spirit. The body is a soil which accepts every seed, a soil in which good and evil can be sown. Thus the good which man has raised in his body, as well as the evil which he has sown in it, follows him in death." Works VII, p. 476. ". . . Before the Fall, since man really stood in closer harmony with the world of spirits, that higher spirit could really have a more immediate influence on him than now. For now, man as he usually is, is too rotten even for the devil. The rottenness is the mixture; sheer evil is, in its way, something pure." Works, VII, p. 479-480.

374 [a] "the able exponent of Plato" is presumably Schleiermacher for whose Addresses on Religion (*Reden über die Religion*) Schelling expressed intense admiration as early as 1801. (See Introduction, section II.) In a letter to August Wilhelm Schlegel, Schelling wrote: "I now honor the author [Schleiermacher] as one who can only be regarded as being exactly on the same level as the greatest and most original philosophers. Without such originality it is impossible to have penetrated the innermost reaches of speculation, without having left behind even a trace of the steps which one had to take . . . He who would produce something of this sort must have undertaken the most profound philosophic studies—or have written with blind, divine inspiration." Letters, I, p. 345.

[b] August Friedrich Böckh published a "specimen edition" of Plato's *Timaeus* which he presented as his dissertation at the University of Heidelberg on November 27th, 1807. Concerning the position of Böckh as a Platonist see the *Philosophische Monatsheft,* 1868, volume I, p. 257 ff.

379 [a] Cf. System of Transcendental Idealism (*System des transcendentalen Idealismus,* 1800, Works, III, pp. 327-634): "Man has a history only because what he will do cannot be anticipated by any theory. Arbitrariness is, insofar, the Goddess of History. Mythology places the beginning of history in the first step out of the rule of instinct into the realm of freedom, in the loss of the Golden Age or in the Fall, that is in the first expression of arbitrariness. According to the ideas of philosophers, history ends in the Realm of Reason, that is in the Golden Age of Right, when all arbitrariness shall have disappeared from earth and man returns through freedom to the same point at which nature originally placed him and which he left when history began." (Works, III, p. 589).

"... We can assume three periods in revelation and thus also three periods in history. The basis for this division is given us by the two opposing factors, Fate and Foresight, in the center between which stands Nature, the transition from one to the other.

"The first period is the one in which the ruling power, as mere fate, that is as altogether blind power, frigidly and unconsciously destroys even the greatest and most glorious things. In this period of history, which we may call the tragic period, there belongs the decline of the radiance and wonder of the ancient world, the fall of those empires of which scarcely a memory remains and whose greatness we may envision only through their ruins, the decline of the noblest humanity which has ever been seen and whose return to earth remains only as an everlasting hope.

"The second period of history is the one in which what appeared in the first as Fate, that is as altogether blind power, reveals itself as Nature. Now the dark law which ruled in the former appears at least transformed into an explicit law of nature, which forces freedom and unrestrained arbitrariness to serve a plan of nature and thus gradually introduces at least a mechanistic lawfulness into history. This period seems to begin with the spread of the great Roman republic. This, insofar as it united the peoples among themselves for the first time, despite expressing the most unrestrained arbitrariness in its general passion of conquest and subjection, brought morals and laws, arts and sciences, which had been preserved separately among distinct peoples, into reciprocal relationship. Unconsciously and even against their will [the nations] were forced to serve a plan of nature which, in its complete development, must bring about the all-inclusive league of peoples, the universal state. Hence all events which occurred in this period are to be regarded as merely natural results, just as even the decline of the Roman Empire itself had neither a tragic nor a moral aspect but was only necessary in accordance with natural law and was really only an offering to nature.

"The third period of history will be the one in which what appeared in the earlier ones as fate and as nature will develop and reveal itself as Foresight. Then that which seemed to be merely the work of fate or nature, will appear as having been the beginning of Foresight revealing itself in incomplete fashion. We cannot say when this period will begin. But when this period comes, then God himself will be." (Works, III, pp. 603-4.)

Cf. also, "Philosophy and Religion": "That condition of unconscious happiness as well as the condition of the primal innocence of the earth, has been preserved in all folk lore in the Myth of the Golden Age. It was natural that the second race of man should thus have immortalized those guardian spirits of its childhood, the benefactors by which it was protected in advance against the future severities of nature by being endowed by instinct with the first arts of life. And having attained the first seeds of science, of religion and of law, it immortalized [these guardian spirits] in the images of the heroes and gods with whom the history of the race everywhere begins in accordance with the traditions of the earliest and most ancient peoples." (Works, VI, p. 59.)

[b] References to disease, here and elsewhere, reflect Schelling's interest in medicine and medical theory. Cf. note a to page 366; also Introduction, section I.

[c] The German conveys more of a balance than the translation can suggest—*Mitteilung* (participation) vs. *Verteilung* (partition) of forces.

381 [a] "the self-centered operation of the basis" as the dark ground of selfhood, seems intended to give a natural basis to egotism rather than to imply any conscious egotism on the part of nature.

[b] "It wishes differentiation": *Er will die Ungleichheit. "Er"* may, of course, refer to God but seems to refer to the "will of the depths" and is therefore translated "it" rather than "he."

389 [a] Cf. Schelling's "System of Philosophy as a Whole" (*System der gesammten Philosophie*) Works, VI, pp. 131-

576): "I admit willingly and gladly to all who wish to assert it, that morality is excluded from my system of philosophy in this sense, as a virtue which an individual can acquire for himself. It is a miserable undertaking to seek to derive God from morality, and not only because so many find the assumption of a God useful as a means towards morality. Such people have a habit of looking at everything from a utilitarian viewpoint. God is for them a household remedy which anyone can use to strengthen himself." Works, VI, p. 557.

390 [a] *Timaeus,* 52b.

392 [a] Cf. "System of Philosophy as a Whole": "True religion is heroism, not an idle brooding, sensitive envisioning or piety. Those are to be called men of God in whom knowledge of God leads directly to action." Works, VI, p. 559.

[b] Cf. "System of Philosophy as a Whole": "By religion . . . I do not mean what is called a sense of the Divine, or piety. He who only has a sense of God is still far removed from God. . . . . Religion is higher than sensing and feeling. The first meaning of this often misused word is conscientiousness; it is the expression of the highest unity of knowledge and action which makes it impossible for one's acts to contradict one's will . . . Even in its origin, religiosity means action being bound, in no wise a choice between opposites as is assumed when the freedom of the will is an *equilibrium arbitrii,* as it is called, but the highest commitment to the right, without choice," Works, VI, p. 558.

394 [a] Cf. Schelling's "On the Nature of Philosophy as Science" (*Über die Natur der Philosophie als Wissenschaft*) Works, IX, pp. 209-246: "He who would place himself at the point of departure of truly free philosophy must leave even God. Here it may be said: He who would save will lose and he who surrenders will find. Only he has delved to the very basis of his being and has recognized the whole depth of his life, who has once forsaken all and been forsaken by all, who has seen all else vanish and beheld himself alone with the Infinite—a tremendous step which Plato compared to death. What Dante saw written on the gates of the Inferno is also to be written, in a different sense, at the entrance to philosophy: Leave all hope behind ye who enter here. He who would truly philosophize must be rid of all hope, all desire, all longing; he must desire nothing, feel himself entirely poor and bereft, surrender all to gain all. This step is hard, the ultimate abnegation. We realize this from the fact that so few have ever been capable of it." (Works, IX, p. 217.)

396 [a] § § 346, 347. The quotation from Leibniz is a free synopsis.

400 [a] It is not clear whether Schelling conceived this intensity as inherent in man or in universal Will. The syntax makes either interpretation possible.

[b] Cf. Psalm 18, 26-27; II Samuel 22, 26-27. Professor J. E. Frame has pointed out to the translator that Luther renders Psalm 18, 27:

Und bei den Reinen bist du rein,

Und bei den Verkehrten bist du verkehrt.

[c] "selfhood . . . brought back from activity to potentiality." *Aktivität zur Potentialität*: from *actuality* to potentiality?

401 [a] J. G. Hamann (1730-1788), the "Wizard of the North," may be considered a forerunner of the German Romantic Movement, and at the same time an advocate of Lutheran mysticism.

Schelling's quotation is from a volume published in 1762 entitled *Kreuzzüge des Philologen* (A Philologist takes up his Cross), published anonymously, but with a sketch and the name "Pan" on the title page. No place of publication was indicated, but it is now known to have been Königsberg.

The citation is from page 196 but not from the section "Cloverleaf of hellenistic Letters" (*Kleeblatt hellenistischer Briefe*) referred to by Schelling. It is from the section entitled "Aesthetica in Nuce—A Rhapsody in Cabbalistic Prose" (*Eine Rhapsodie in Kabalıstische Prosa*). Cf. the collection of Hamann's writings (*Hamann's Schriften*) edited by Friedrich Roth, Berlin 1821, volume II, p. 286. The parenthesis—"*the devil's*"—is Schelling's.

On January 5, 1809 Schelling wrote to Friedrich Roth: "How can I thank you enough, most respected sir, . . . for the collection of Hamann's letters and the biography with the introduction to the Biblical Commentary. To you alone I am indebted for the fact that I have come to understand this Wizard and Prophet far better than I ever would have been able to from his writings. Not without shame for having kept them so long I send you back these glorious works." (Letters II, pp. 146-7.)

In his essay "On the Relation of the creative Arts to Nature" (*Über das Verhältnis der bildenden Künste zu der Natur,* Works, VII, pp. 289-329) Schelling wrote: "It would be strange indeed if the very ones who deny all life to nature, set it up to be copied in art. To them are applicable the words of that profound man, J. G. Hamann in the 'Cloverleaf of hellenistic Letters' II, page 189. [The quotation is actually from Hamann's '*Aesthetica in Nuce*']: 'Your lying philosophy has cleared Nature out of the way and why do you demand that we copy it? So that you can renew the pleasure of carrying out the same acts of violence on the students of nature?' These words have been modified in the context of the present speech, for in the man's own phrasing they are as follows: 'A murderous, lying philosophy has cleared Nature out of the way, and why do you demand that we copy it? So that you can renew the pleasure by being the murderers of the students of nature?'—If only F. H. Jacobi to whom the author is indebted for his first more exact acquaintance with the writings of that spirit of primal power, would either undertake the long hoped for edition of Hamann's works himself, or else hasten it through his influence." (Works, VII, pp. 293-294.)

In his notes "On the History of Modern Philosophy" (*Zur Geschichte der neueren Philosophie,* Works, X, pp. 1-200) Schelling said of Hamann's works that these "writings which were formerly scattered like sibylline leaves . . . are, without any question, the most important enrichment which literature has recently received . . . a many-sided learning is required to understand their manifold allusions, and a more profound experience to grasp their whole significance. They are not reading matter for youths but for men, writings which a man should never lay aside, which he should constantly regard as touchstones of his own understanding . . .

"Hamann had no system and did not set one up. But one could say to oneself that one had reached a degree of insight, insofar as a human being can lay claim to understanding, if one were conscious of a whole and had drawn together in a single comprehension all Hamann's various and disparate expressions, the consistent and the apparently inconsistent, the utterly free and, on the other hand, the crudely orthodox utterances. Philosophy is really a profound science, a work of great experience. People who lack experience, mere technicians, can accomplish nothing here even if they have the right in passing judgment on Hamann to reveal their own characters, when, since they are unable to penetrate the essence of his form of thought, they restrict themselves to his personal faults and weaknesses. Without these, moreover, the man would hardly have been this man; and these faults and weaknesses are so connected with the virtues and merits of his spirit that they cannot be separated from them." (Works, X, pp. 170-1.)

402 [a] § 25. In Leibniz' text the sentences read: Ex quo concludendum est, Deum antecedenter velle omne bonum in se, velle consequenter optimum, tanquam finem, velle id, quod indifferens est, et malum physicum interdum tanquam medium, sed velle duntaxat permittere malum morale, tanquam conditionem, sine qua non obtineretur optimum, ita nimirum, ut malum non, nisi titulo necessitatis hypotheticae, id ipsum cum optimo connectentis admittatur. (p. 139, § 25.)

Quod ad vitium adtinet, superius ostensum est, illud

non esse objectum decreti divini, tanquam medium, sed tanquam conditionem sine qua non; et ideo duntaxat permitti. (p. 292, § 230.)

404 [a] Cf. Hebrews 1, 1-2. But the "realization" is not here postponed to a "distant future."

[b] The passage referred to reads: "Just as the final purpose of history is the atonement of that which had fallen, so the latter may be regarded from a positive point of view. For the first selfhood of the Ideas was one which had its source in the immediate acts of God; but the selfhood and absoluteness into which they enter through atonement is given in itself, so that they exist in the Absolute independently and autonomously. Thus the Fall becomes the means of God's completed Revelation. Since God, by reason of the eternal necessity of his nature, endows his vision with selfhood, he himself gives it finitude and sacrifices it, as it were, so that the Ideas which existed in him without a life of their own, are called to life but just on this account become capable of again entering into Absoluteness as independent entities." (Works, VI, p. 63. Erroneously indicated as "IV, p. 63" in VII, p. 404.)

405 [a b c] I Corinthians 15, 25-28; Mark 12, 36; Psalms 110.

407 [a] On the distinction between Being as existence and Being as the basis of existence, see page 357.

408 [a] In Schelling's Works, VII, pp. 140-197, the title is: "Aphorisms introductory to the Philosophy of Nature" (*Aphorismen zur Einleitung in die Naturphilosophie*) Aphorisms 162 and 163 here appear on page 174.

"162. The difference between a divine and a merely finite Identity is that in the former it is not those opposing factors which require connection that are combined, but rather those of which each could exist independently and yet does not attain being without the other.

"163. This is the secret of eternal Love—that that which would fain be absolute in itself nonetheless does not regard it as a deprivation to be so in itself but is so only in and with another. If each entity were not a Whole but only a part of the Whole there would be no Love: Since each is a Whole and nonetheless does not exist and cannot be without the other—thence there is Love."

Cf. aphorism 215 and footnote on page 186.

409 [a] This reference should be to the "Heidelberg Literary Annuals" (*Heidelberger Jahrbücher der Literatur*) for 1808, volume I, section 5 (Philology, history, literature and art), part 2, page 242. This is part of a review of the second—enlarged and revised—edition of "Lectures on German Science and Literature" (*Vorlesungen über die deutsche Wissenschaft und Literatur*) by Adam H. Müller, Dresden, 1807. The review is unsigned but in the table of contents is credited to "Fr. S." The paragraph referred to by Schelling reads: "It is a sight which fills one partly with astonishment, partly with melancholy, to behold the history of the last century, so full of destruction, pregnant with ominous signs. For one sees the leading German minds for close to fifty years and almost without exception totally lost in a merely aesthetic view of things. One beholds almost all busying themselves with this aesthetic view until finally every serious view of God and country, every recollection of ancient fame was extinguished up to the last trace, and with them the spirit of strength and loyalty. There were always individuals more seriously minded, who knew a higher inspiration than mere aesthetics; but what could individuals do against the stream? The aesthetic view is one founded essentially in the spirit of man; but when it rules exclusively and alone, it becomes an irresponsible dream life and, however sublimated, leads at most to that destructive pantheistic bunkum which we now see not only in academic hair splitting but ruling almost universally in a thousand varying and footloose forms. This is really the evil which is consuming the best powers of the German heart and is finally corrupting men to the point of unfeeling indifference. This aesthetic dream life, this unmanly, pantheistic bunkum, this playing with distinctions must cease; they are unworthy of this great age and unfitting. The sense of art and feeling for nature will surely remain with us as long as we are Germans; but the

power and seriousness of truth, firm consideration for God and for our vocation must claim first place and again assume its ancient rights as befits the German character."

411 [a] Cf. Romans 8, 18(?)

413 [a] "Paganism, taken historically, is as original as Christianity." The text reads *"Heiligtum"* (sanctuary) but this would seem to be a misprint for *Heidentum* (paganism).

414 [a] The essay here referred to, "On the Analogy between the Instinct to Know and the Reproductive Instinct" (*Über die Analogie des Erkenntnis und des Zeugungs Triebes*) appears in Baader's Collected Works (*Sämmtliche Werke*) edited by Dr. Franz Hoffmann, Leipzig 1851, volume I pp. 38-49; and also in Baader's Writings (*Schriften*) selected and edited by Max Pulver, Leipzig, 1921, pp. 31-38. Numerous footnotes which appeared in the original were not reprinted.

415 [a] Cf. Schelling's Stuttgart Lectures: "The essence of the soul is also love, and love, too, is the principle of all which arises out of the soul.—It is generally recognized that a radiant atmosphere of love must envelop and transfigure a work of art. We say of the most beautiful objects that they were created with love, yes that love made them.—Science too, in its highest incarnation is a work of love, and therefore rightly bears the lovely name Philosophy, that is, love of wisdom." (Works, VII, p. 474).

[b] The tradition to which reason "was referred earlier" would seem to be scholasticism. See Schelling's own, later comment in his "Philosophy of Revelation" (*Philosophie der Offenbarung,* Works 2, III and IV): "Throughout the middle ages mystical teachings went alongside scholasticism which held sway in the schools and was approved by the Church; [these mystical teachings] asserted themselves right into the age of the Reformation, following which they reappeared and attained their pinnacle in Jacob Böhme . . . Up to now Philosophy has been unable to achieve in a scientific way, convincing to reason, what these mystical teachings sought or claimed to achieve, indeed only in unscientific ways. For this very reason these teachings

imply the necessity of a Positive Philosophy even if they do not realize it themselves." (Works 2, III, pp. 119-120.)

In connection with the foregoing and with section V of the Introduction, see also the following lines from Schelling's work on "The World Ages" (*Die Weltalter,* Works, VIII, pp. 195-344): "Here runs the boundary between theosophy and philosophy which he who loves science will seek to preserve undefiled. The former (theosophy) has as many advantages in depth, abundance and vitality of content over the latter (philosophy) as the real object has over its reproduction, nature over its representation. And indeed this difference reaches the point of incommensurability if a dead philosophy is taken for comparison, one which seeks the essence of things only in forms and concepts. Hence the preference of profound spirits for theosophy, a preference just as readily explicable as a preference for nature in contrast to art." (Works, VIII, p. 204.)

[c] The furthering of poetry "through a study of the writings of all nations"—by Herder, the Grimms, and others.

416 [a] This promise was never fulfilled. See Introduction, section I.

BIBLIOGRAPHY

Editions of *Philosophische Untersuchungen über das Wesen der menschlichen Freiheit und die damit zusammenhängenden Gegenstände.*

1. *F. W. J. Schellings philosophische Schriften. Erster Band* (Landshut, Philipp Krüll, Universitätsbuchhändler, 1809) pp. vii-xii; 397-511.
2. Reprint, (Reutlingen, J. N. Ensslinschen Buchhandlung, 1834). First separate publication of the *Inquiries.*
3. *Friedrich Wilhelm Joseph von Schellings Sämmtliche Werke. VII Band, I Abteilung,* 1805-1810. Edited by K. F. A. Schelling (Stuttgart & Augsburg, J. G. Cotta, 1860) pp. 333-416.
4. *F. W. J. Schellings Werke. III Band.* Edited by Otto Weiss (Leipzig, Felix Meiner, 1911) pp. 427-512.
5. Edited by Christian Herrmann, with introduction and index (Leipzig, Felix Meiner, 1925).
6. Edited by J. Rodenberg (Hannover, Banas & Dette).
7. *Schellings Werke: Münchner Jubiläumsdruck. IV Hauptband: Schriften zur Philosophie der Freiheit,* 1804-1815. Rearranged and edited by Manfred Schröter (München, C. H. Beck & R. Oldenbourg, 1927) pp. 223-308.
8. *Fr. Wilhelm Schellings Schöpferisches Handeln.* Edited by Emil Fuchs (Jena & Leipzig, Eugen Diederichs, 1907). Extensive selections from the *Inquiries,* pp. 215-293.
9. *Ricerche filosofiche su la essenza della libertá umana e gli ogetti che vi si collegano di F. W. J. Schelling.* Translation, introduction and notes by Michele Losacco (Lanciano, Carabba, 1910).
10. *Recherches philosophiques sur l'essence de la liberté humaine.* Translation by Georges Politzer (Paris, Henri Lefebvre, 1926).

Commentaries on the *Inquiries*

"Eschenmayer an Schelling, über dessen Abhandlung: Philosophische Untersuchungen über das Wesen der menschlichen Freyheit." *Allgemeine Zeitschrift von Deutschen für Deutsche herausgegeben von Schelling, I Band, i Heft* (Nürnberg, Johann Leonhard Schrag, 1813) pp. 79-129. (Reprinted in Schelling's *Werke,* VIII, pp. 145-160, together with Schelling's reply, pp. 161-189.)

Friedrich Frederichs: *Über den Schelling'schen Freiheitsbegriff* (Halle, Pfeffer, 1890).

Wilhelm Greiner: *Das Problem der menschlichen Willensfreiheit bei Kant und Schelling.*=Jahresbericht des Grossherzoglichen Realgymnasiums (Eisenach, 1909-11).

Friedrich Groos: *Die Schelling'sche Gottes und Freiheitslehre vor den Richterstuhl der gesunden Vernunft vorgefordert.* (Tübingen, Heinrich Laupp, 1819).

Francois Maugé: "La liberté dans l'idéalisme transcendantal de Schelling." *Archiv für Geschichte der Philosophie,* 14 (Berlin, 1901) pp. 361-383; 517-535.

F. G. Süsskind: "Prüfung der Schellingschen Lehren von Gott, Weltschöpfung, Freiheit." *Flatts Magazin für christliche Dogmatik und Moral* (Tübingen, 1812) pp. 1 *ff.*

———: *Über das Wesen der menschlichen Freiheit. Zur Erläuterung und Würdigung der Schelling'schen Theorie, diese Lehre betrachtend* (Leipzig, Voss, 1821).

Johann Eduard Erdmann: "Schellings Freiheitslehre." *Grundriss der Geschichte der Philosophie, II Band* (4 ed., Berlin, 1896) pp. 575-582.

Attention may also be directed to chapters on Schelling and treatments of his "Philosophy of Freedom" in Histories of Philosophy such as those of Fischer, Hartmann, Windelband, Zeller, etc. referred to in the Introduction and Notes to the present volume, e.g. Kuno Fischer's *Geschichte der Philosophie, VII Band: Schellings Leben, Werke und Lehre* (3 ed., Heidelberg, 1902) pp. 633-668.

In addition to other special treatments cited in the Introduction and Notes, such as those by Beckers, Dilthey, Heine, Royce, Stefansky, etc., attention may also be called to Rudolf Haym's *Die romantische Schule* (4 ed., Berlin, 1920) and to Hinrich Knittermeyer's *Schelling und die romantische Schule* (München, 1929).

In this connection there may also be mentioned, in addition to Schelling's Letters cited above, *Aus Schellings Leben. In Briefen,* three volumes edited by G. L. Plitt (Leipzig, 1869-1870), *Aus Schellings Nachlass. Neue Briefe*, edited by Otto Braun (Leipzig, 1911).

Schelling Bibliographies

James Mark Baldwin: *Dictionary of Philosophy and Psychology.* (New York & London, 1905) vol. III, 1, pp. 453 *ff*.

Friedrich Ueberweg: *Grundriss der Geschichte der Philosophie. IV Teil. Die deutsche Philosophie des neunzehnten Jahrhunderts und der Gegenwart.* 12 ed. edited by Traugott Konstantin Oesterreich (Berlin, 1923) pp. 674-677. *Cf.* also pp. 35-67.

Joh. Jost: *F. W. J. Schelling. Bibliographie der Schriften von ihm und über ihn.* (Bonn, 1927).

Rowland Gray-Smith: Bibliography supplementary to Jost's in *God in the Philosophy of Schelling* (Philadelphia, 1933) pp. 117-120.

Addenda to Jost's and Gray-Smith's Bibliographies

1901 Francois Maugé: "La liberté dans l'idéalisme transcendantal de Schelling." *Archiv für Geschichte der Philosophie,* 14 (Berlin) pp. 361-383; 517-535.

1928 Erich Becher: *Fr. W. J. Schelling.* Reprint from *Friedrich Manns Pädagogisches Magazin,* No. 1184 (Langensalza).

Kurt Sternberg: "Schelling, der Philosoph der Romantik." *Archiv für Rechts und Wirtschaftsphilosophie,* 22 (Berlin) pp. 535-543.

1929 Erich Becher: *Deutsche Philosophen; Lebensgang und Lehrgebäude von Kant, Schelling, Fechner, Lotze, Lange, Erdmann, Mach, Stumpf, Bäumker, Eucken, Siegfried Becher* (München & Leipzig).

1930 Gerbrand Jan Dekker: *Die Rückwendung zum Mythos; Schellings letzte Wandlung* (München & Berlin).

1931 Hermann Zeltner: *Schellings philosophische Idee und das Identitätssystem* (Heidelberg).

1932 Paul Kluckhohn: *Weltanschauung der Frühromantik* (Leipzig).

1933 Christoph Ertel: "Schellings positive Philosophie, ihr Werden und Wesen." *Philosophisches Jahrbuch der Görres Gesellschaft,* 47 (Fulda) pp. 84-112.

Rowland Gray-Smith: *God in the Philosophy of Schelling* (Philadelphia).

Herman Hausheer: "Thought affinities of Schelling and Bergson." *Personalist,* 14 (Los Angeles) pp. 93-106.

Vladimir Jankélévitch: *L'Odyssée de la conscience dans la dernière philosophie de Schelling* (Paris).

Hildegard Schrader: *Das Wesen des Schönen bei Schelling im Vergleich zu Kants Kritik der Urteilskraft* (Braunschweig).

1934 Maximilian Beck "Kritik der Schelling-Jaspers-Heideggerschen Ontologie." *Philosophische Hefte,* 4 (Prag) pp. 97-164.

Jonas Cohn: "Potenz und Existenz, eine Studie über Schellings letzte Philosophie." *Joel Festschrift* (Basel) pp. 44-69.

Karl Eswein: *Schellings Verhältnis zu Aristoteles* (Fulda).

Jean Gibelin: *L'esthétique de Schelling et l'Allemagne de Madame de Staël* (Paris).

Otto Kein: *Die Universitalität des Geistes im Lebenswerk Goethes und Schellings* (Berlin).

Max Koppel: "Schellings Einfluss auf die Naturphilosophie Görres." *Philosophisches Jahrbuch der Görres Gesellschaft,* 47 (Fulda) pp. 220-244, 346-369.

Kurt Schilling: *Natur und Wahrheit. Untersuchung über Entwicklung des Schellingschen Systems bis* 1800 (München).

Manfred Schröter: "Historische Übersicht über die Schelling-literatur." *Idealismus,* 1 (Zürich) pp. 219-227.

INDEX